W9-BSD-873

Books of Merit

Georgian Bay Gourmet Entertains

Georgian Bay Gourmet Entertains

Anne Connell

Helen Gibson

Mary Hunt

Jean Leavens

Thomas Allen Publishers

Toronto

Copyright © 2000 by Anne Connell, Helen Gibson,
Mary Hunt, and Jean Leavens

All rights reserved. No part of this work may be reproduced or
transmitted in any form or by any means—graphic, electronic or mechanical,
including photocopying, recording, taping or information storage and
retrieval systems—without the prior written permission of the publisher,
or in the case of photocopying or other reprographic copying,
a license from the Canadian Copyright Licensing Agency.

Canadian Cataloguing in Publication Data

Main entry under title:

Georgian Bay Gourmet Entertains

ISBN 0-919028-39-X

1. Cookery.   2. Menus.   I. Connell, Anne.

TX714.G46 2000   641.5   C00-931497-0

Editors: Lenore d'Anjou and Shaun Oakey
Front cover photograph: Joy von Tiedemann
Back cover and inside photographs: Hudson Leavens
Author photograph: Hudson Leavens

Published by Thomas Allen Publishers,
a division of Thomas Allen & Son Limited
145 Front Street East, Suite 107
Toronto, Ontario M5A 1E3 Canada

Printed and bound in Canada

This book is dedicated to

Chris, Anne, Hugh, Jessica, Ed, Grace,
Lindsay, John and Tony

Contents

CHAPTER SIX: WINTER

Introduction

"We define gourmet food as the end result rather than the method, because we, like most of you, enjoy good food but lack the time to spend in the kitchen."
– Georgian Bay Gourmets, May 1983

*A*S TRUE TODAY as it was then. Almost twenty years ago, we wrote and self-published two cookbooks that became Canadian best-sellers. They were called *Georgian Bay Gourmet Winter Entertaining* and *Georgian Bay Gourmet Summer Entertaining*. We found ourselves travelling to western Canada on three different occasions for book signings and cooking demonstrations. We were featured in *Canadian Living*, *Chatelaine* and *Maclean's* magazines; we were interviewed by Peter Gzowski, Joe Cote on CBC, and by Betty Kennedy; we cooked with Don Herron, Betty Thompson and Margaret Trudeau. Our books were featured in Canadian Living's *The History of Cooking in Canada* as two of a selection of cookbooks chosen as the most popular in the 1980s. These were exciting times for four young women from central Ontario! Interesting to note that, while our books were about living near Georgian Bay, the largest sales were in Vancouver and throughout the Ottawa region.

The inspiration behind our books came, very simply, from our love for cooking and entertaining, which filled a large part of each of our lives in this beautiful place. Throughout the books we traced the four seasons as we experienced them in "Georgian Bay territory," we talked about our interests and the activities characteristic of each season, and we designed menus with good home cooking that centred around these activities.

Our books were among the first to offer a menu format. It was our belief—and it still is—that most cooks can follow a basic recipe. However, our friends had told us they wanted to learn how to put foods and recipes together in ways that would be nutritionally well balanced, complementary in flavour and pleasing to the eye. So our menus offered a variety of creative ideas, with easily found ingredients. They were not labour intensive and often appealed to the cook on the run. Our readers told us that they loved our format—along with the photographs that illustrated the character and beauty of Georgian Bay.

Needless to say, we're back, twenty years later! We must now live with the realization that we are middle-aged women—but in all this time, our friendship has remained ever-present, and we still share our enthusiasm for cooking and entertaining in the place we love to live. We continue to take part in most of those wonderful outdoor activities that the Georgian Bay area has to offer—we just don't do it as quickly! Our children have all grown up, and so we find we cook differently. We plan home-coming feasts when the kids visit from university, and then create those wonderful romantic dinners for two when they've all gone back! Georgian Bay winters are still too long, but good food and good friends have always brought warmth to those cold and blustery nights. And glorious Georgian Bay summers will always give cause to celebrate, if only for the fact that we are still fortunate enough to live here and experience them every year.

But twenty years has also made us, each in our own way, learn how to combine the good life with more sensible eating.

While we do not present ourselves as nutritionists, we have discovered within ourselves the ability to create and recreate recipes with good health in mind. In this book, we continue to offer all the "good stuff"—all the good, down-to-earth recipes from our mothers and grandmothers, presented in menu format, in harmony with the joys of each season and living near Georgian Bay. We have included some old favourites (which of course have been revised), and we introduce a variety of new and delicious taste treats that, by virtue of good flavour alone, will overshadow the fact that they are healthy and nutritious. We do not preach about cholesterol or low-fat foods, but we gently guide our readers into a more sensible way of cooking great food.

And so, you ask, what have we been up to in the past twenty years?

Anne continues to be our creative culinary genius. Using the herbs and vegetables from Herb's organic garden, she is applauded by her family and friends for many memorable culinary creations. She also blends enthusiasm and concern for the nutritional needs of her long-distance runner husband (that's Herb; he's retired now). Though Anne says that the most important aspect of her life is her family, she also shares her great spirit and boundless energy with the students of her Life Skills class at a local high school. As she plans for her daughter's wedding, she readily admits that the birthday parties of years gone by were a heck of a lot easier.

Gone are the days when we can refer to her as Nurse Jean or Real Estate Jean, since Jean now owns and operates a camera and framing shop in downtown Midland with her husband, Photographer Hudson. Jean especially loves to tell the tales of her three grown children, who all travel the world with their work interests and exotic holidays. For those infrequent but very special times when they are all at home under one roof, Jean will cook up a storm (but is it really true that they all love tofu and all those funny-looking beans?). We are happy to report that Jean has finally solved the mystery of static cling, but is still cursing the reality of broken nails.

Then there's Mary, who for twenty years has maintained the calm and stability of the group—or something like that! Her copious notes and revisions, and her attention to detail, have made her the backbone of this project. However, the rewards of a working life await her as she gears up for retirement in 2002, and she will probably pursue her great love for travel. No doubt husband Ron will tag along, making sure there is a Harrier run at each destination. Mary says that now that the kids are all in university, she has replaced child-rearing with physical fitness. If you can't find her at home, you'll find her in a workout at the Y.

And finally, Helen. "My family is like a rich and flavourful recipe: Take one wonderful partner and add to him two outstanding sons, three amazing stepchildren, one beautiful daughter-in-law, one delightful son-in-law, two adorable girlfriends, and one very gorgeous grandchild … so far!" While Helen has never in twenty years allowed the cookbook girls to forget that she is the youngest of the group, she has no qualms about becoming the first grandmother. When the whole family is around, the same question usually surfaces at dinnertime: "Are we going to be guinea pigs tonight?" (The jury is still out on the chicken burgers.) Outside of her family, Helen takes pride in recently passing the Canadian Securities Course for her new career in the investment business.

In our efforts to produce this book, we are especially happy to acknowledge that as a group of four goods friends, twenty years has not diminished our combined sense of humour, nor has it exhausted our creative energies as a team. We may be saying "Goodbye, heavy cream; so long, salted butter; and adios, deep-fried anything," but we're having fun! What a perfect time in our lives . . . when fibre is near and dear to our hearts, when low-fat foods digest more efficiently, and when sensible eating allows us to control the middle-age spread. How wonderful that we are still the Georgian Bay Gourmets—just a little bit older, and somewhat wiser!

Thanks to our guys for sticking by us, and thanks to our friend Gloria Dubeau for all her help.

Shopping Notes

WHEN YOU DECIDE to change your eating habits, take some time and go to your grocery store, deli and health food store. Don't shop—just go up and down the aisles and browse and read labels. See what is available—there is a whole new world of food waiting for you. Learn how to read food labels, so you can spot hidden fats, sodium levels, cholesterol, saturated fats. You may still decide to buy and eat the foods you've always (guiltily?) enjoyed, but at least now you will know what you are eating.

Try to substitute lower-fat items in your present recipes to start, or try some of ours.

Some suggested items to buy:

Pantry Items

- brown rice and wild rice
- split peas and chickpeas
- lentils
- varieties of beans, canned or dry
  (Black beans and kidney beans are particularly good.)
- Dijon mustard
- vinegars
- olive oil or other pan coating sprays

- olive oil
- egg whites and egg substitutes
- evaporated skim milk or skim milk powder
- skim milk or no more than 1% milk
- fat-free mayonnaise—try different brands until you find one you like
- no-fat sour cream
- no-fat yogurt, plain or fruit
- vegetable stock mix
- light and/or low-sodium soy sauce
- salt substitute
- pasta (Try soba or buckwheat pasta. The taste is remarkable and it is very healthy.)
- canned tomatoes, sauce and paste
- unsweetened applesauce—a substitute for butter and oil in baking.

Soya Products

- Textured Vegetable Protein (TVP) can be added to spaghetti sauces, stews and soups to add protein.
- Veggie Ground Round is a fat-free substitute for ground beef. It can be used in meat loaf, lasagna or any recipe that calls for ground beef.
- Veggie Slices substitute for cheese. They taste great on sandwiches and casseroles and they melt nicely.
- Veggie Burgers and Soya Jumbo Dogs taste great when barbecued and dressed with your favourite condiments.
- Veggie Pepperoni Slices. Try these on your next pizza—they taste just like the real thing!

Bread and Rolls

- Choose whole grain bread and rolls to make a complete protein. If the protein in your meal comes from beans or other vegetable products, you need to add a whole grain product to make the protein complete.

Georgian Bay Gourmet Entertains

1

Spring

~~~~~~~~~~~~~~~~

Asian Spring

Oceans Alive

Spring Fling

Four Ladies and a Lunch

Chili on the Run

Rise and Shine Brunch

Opening Up the Cottage

Victoria Day Blast

Spring Fry

*T*HROUGHOUT GEORGIAN BAY, springtime signals a revival of all the forces of life. *Printemps*, as they say in neighbouring Lafontaine, develops slowly and teases us with brilliant warm days followed by sudden grey snow squalls. Nevertheless, the fertile earth is gently encouraging the first wild bloodroot and snowdrops.

The black ice in the Bay heaves in the southerly breezes and slowly pulls away from the rocky shores. And then, as if by magic, the fractured ice pack slips away and disappears in the great blue expanse of Lake Huron.

Springtime in Georgian Bay often seems to arrive in April, but the real awakening occurs with maple syrup time. Frosty nights followed by sparkly days is the formula for "sugaring off." Plastic tubing loops from tree to tree to collect the sap, which is then evaporated to produce sultry amber maple syrup. In April the many sugar bushes near the Bay attract the first visitors. It's worth the hike into the bush to sniff the sweet steam in the evaporator houses. The Elmvale Maple Syrup Festival is always a family favourite to celebrate this springtime event, and the horses and wagons are still on hand to take young and old alike out to the sugar bush. Throughout our book, you will find that we have chosen the deliciously natural flavour of maple syrup as the sweetener for many of our desserts.

As April progresses, the sense of awakening is accelerated by the lengthening days. It's finally time to bring out our bikes and warm up our running shoes. After our typically long winters, we are eager to get out and get moving.

The mystical loons have migrated from their winter ranges to the sparkling waters of our Bay. Late at night and very early in the morning, their eerie cries excite the unsuspecting shoredweller. Tiny flocks of colourful ducks splash down on the still water—buffleheads and scaups from the Atlantic flyway. And soon, the drone of an outboard motor is heard as a fisherman ventures out on a perch-catching expedition.

The finishing touch to the seasonal revival is the planting of gardens. Nurseries and landscape centres are abustle with eager gardeners. Rows of bedding plants and racks of seeds feed the dreams for the greenthumb set. Rock gardens are cleared of winter debris, and clumps of pansies, geraniums and impatiens are set out. The very latest in tomato varieties are staked, and fresh herbs are given their rightful place of honour in the cook's garden. And so the Georgian Bay spring is in full swing!

Then, suddenly, the sweet spell of spring is broken by the flurry of our returning students. It seems like only yesterday that a beautiful spring day would bring them through the door in muddy rubber boots, nets and jars in dirty little hands, after a busy afternoon of spring dipping at the Wye Marsh. Now they are home and the house is filled with the happy sounds of family—the telephone ringing, the washing machine rumbling, the fridge door swinging, the wonderful stories and lively conversation.

Our spring section has a flair of its own. We've included those seasonal favourites that are sure to please: local asparagus in our Honey-Sesame Asparagus recipe, and the wonderful flavour of our garden rhubarb in Bananas with Rhubarb Sauce and Strawberry-Rhubarb Tango. Introduce your family and friends to falafels, and don't forget the Tzatziki Sauce. After a busy day of opening up the cottage, our Traditional Veggie Lasagna can't be beat, and treat your Easter weekend company to our Rise and Shine Brunch.

Get ready—let's bring on summer!

Asian Spring

FOR 8

Cindy Lou's Spicy Chicken Curry

(White Rice)

(Naan Bread)

Stir-Fry Broccoli

Lemon-Lime Sorbet

Cindy Lou's Spicy Chicken Curry

SERVES 8

2 tbsp.	olive oil	30 mL
1½ cups	sliced onions	375 mL
4	boneless, skinless chicken breasts, cut into bite-sized pieces	4
4	cloves garlic, minced	4
1½ cups	chopped celery	375 mL
1 tbsp.	finely chopped fresh ginger	15 mL
2 tsp.	ground coriander	10 mL
2 tsp.	ground cumin	10 mL
1 tsp.	Asian chili powder (2 tsp / 10 mL for hotter curry)	5 mL
1 tsp.	salt	5 mL
½ tsp.	turmeric	2 mL
3	whole cloves	3
2	cardamom pods	2
2-inch	cinnamon stick	5 cm
3 cups	canned diced tomatoes	750 mL
1½ cups	sliced mushrooms	375 mL

Condiments

3	bananas, sliced	3
1 cup	peanuts	250 mL
2	large tomatoes, diced	2

1. In a large frying pan or wok, heat the oil. Stir-fry onions for 10 minutes or until golden.
2. Add chicken and garlic. Stir-fry until chicken is cooked through. Add the celery and continue to stir-fry.
3. Combine fresh ginger and other spices thoroughly. Add to the pan, stirring to coat the chicken with spices.
4. Add the tomatoes and mushrooms. Transfer the mixture to a larger pan if needed. Cover and cook over medium heat for 20 minutes.
5. Serve over white rice. Pass the condiments in separate bowls at the table.

Preparation Note

Asian chili powder is made from small dried red chili peppers and is very hot. It is different from the Mexican chili powder we use in such dishes as chili con carne.

To allow the flavours to marry, prepare the day before. Just reheat over medium heat.

Stir-Fry Broccoli

SERVES 8

~~~~~~~~~~~~~~~~~~~~~~~~~~~~~

2	bunches broccoli	2
1 tbsp.	canola oil	15 mL
2	cloves garlic, minced	2
1½ cups	sliced celery	375 mL
½ tsp.	salt	2 mL
½ tsp.	grated fresh ginger	2 mL
4 tbsp.	water	60 mL

1. Cut broccoli flowerets and stems into 2-inch (5cm) pieces.
2. Heat oil in a large frying pan or wok and add garlic. Stir-fry for 1 minute.
3. Add broccoli and celery and stir-fry for about 3 minutes.
4. Add salt, ginger and water. Cover and steam for 2 or 3 minutes or until broccoli is cooked but still crisp.
5. Serve immediately.

Lemon-Lime Sorbet

SERVES 8

1¼ cups	sugar	300 mL
¼ cup	corn syrup	50 mL
4 cups	water	1 L
	Juice of 6 lemons	
	Juice of 2 limes	
2 tsp.	grated lemon zest	10 mL
	Mint sprigs for garnish	

1. Heat sugar, corn syrup and water in a saucepan over high heat, stirring occasionally, until mixture boils and sugar dissolves. Remove from heat.
2. Add the juices and zest. Stir.
3. Pour mixture into a 9- x 9-inch (2.5 L) metal baking pan. Cover with foil. Freeze until at least partially frozen (3 hours or overnight).
4. Break mixture into pieces. Blend in a food processor until smooth. Return mixture to the pan; cover and freeze at least 3 more hours.
5. To serve, remove from freezer at least 15 minutes before serving. Spoon into glass serving dishes. Garnish with a sprig of mint.

Preparation Note

Can be prepared a day or two ahead.

Oceans Alive

FOR 6

Smoked Salmon Wraps

*Scallops and Pasta in
Roasted Red Pepper Sauce*

Mediterranean Salad

Savoury French Bread

Poached Pears with Raspberry Sauce

Smoked Salmon Wraps

SERVES 6 TO 8

4	large soft tortillas (flavoured or plain)	4
8 oz.	light cream cheese	250 g
¼ cup	finely chopped green onions	50 mL
4 tbsp.	chopped fresh dill	60 mL
1 bag (10 oz.)	fresh spinach	1 bag (284 g)
1 pkg. (10.6 oz.)	sliced smoked salmon	1 pkg. (300 g)
	Juice of 1 lemon	
	Black pepper to taste	

1. Spread tortillas with cream cheese.
2. Sprinkle with green onions and dill.
3. Layer spinach leaves over top, followed by strips of smoked salmon.
4. Drizzle with lemon juice and sprinkle with black pepper.
5. Roll up tortillas; seal in plastic wrap. Chill several hours.
6. To serve, slice each roll into rounds.

Preparation Note

If you do not like smoked salmon, a good substitute is black forest ham.

Scallops and Pasta in Roasted Red Pepper Sauce

SERVES 6

12 oz.	angel hair pasta	375 g
2 cups	evaporated milk	500 mL
1 cup	drained roasted red peppers (from a jar)	250 mL
¼ cup	vodka (optional)	50 mL
1 tsp.	salt	5 mL
½ tsp.	pepper	2 mL
½ cup	all-purpose flour	125 mL
1½ lb.	scallops, rinsed and dried	750 g
2 tbsp.	light butter	30 mL
1	medium onion, chopped	1
3	cloves garlic, minced	3
3 tbsp.	chopped fresh parsley	45 mL

1. Cook pasta according to package directions. Drain and set aside.
2. In blender, purée evaporated milk, peppers, vodka (if desired), half of the salt and half of the pepper.
3. Combine flour with remaining salt and pepper; coat scallops in flour mixture.

4. In a large skillet, melt butter over high heat. Add onion and garlic; cook until golden brown, about 5 minutes.
5. Add scallops and cook, stirring often, until golden, about 3 minutes. Remove from skillet. Cover to keep warm.
6. Add pepper mixture to skillet; cook until liquid is reduced by a third (about 3 minutes).
7. Toss pasta and scallops with sauce.
8. Sprinkle with parsley and serve immediately.

Mediterranean Salad

SERVES 6 TO 8

~~~~~~~~~~~~~~~~~~~~

1	large head romaine	1
3	tomatoes, cut in wedges	3
2	stalks celery, diced	2
1	cucumber, sliced	1
1	red onion, sliced in rings	1
½ cup	sliced black olives	125 mL
¼ cup	chopped green onions	50 mL
¼ cup	crumbled feta cheese	50 mL
	Mediterranean Dressing (below)	

1. Tear lettuce into a large bowl. Add the remaining ingredients and toss.
2. Dress with Mediterranean Dressing just before serving.

Mediterranean Dressing

Yields ½ cup/125 mL

3 tbsp.	olive oil	45 mL
3 tbsp.	red wine vinegar	45 mL
2 tbsp.	water	30 mL
½ tsp.	dried oregano	2 mL
2	cloves garlic, minced	2
	Salt and pepper to taste	

1. Put all ingredients in a jar and shake to mix.

Savoury French Bread

～～～～～～～～～

Oven: 400°F/200°C

1	large loaf French bread	1
¼ cup	low-fat margarine, softened	50 mL
1 tsp.	dried basil	5 mL
1 tsp.	dried chives	5 mL
1 tsp.	garlic powder	5 mL
½ tsp.	paprika	2 mL

1. Slice bread diagonally without cutting through bottom crust.
2. Mix remaining ingredients and spread between bread slices.
3. Wrap loaf in foil. Heat in oven 15 to 20 minutes. Serve warm.

Poached Pears with Raspberry Sauce

SERVES 6

~~~~~~~~~~~~~~~~~~~~~~~~

10 cups	water	2.5 L
½ cup	sugar	125 mL
	Grated zest and juice of 1 lemon	
½ tsp.	vanilla	2 mL
6	pears, peeled with stems left on	6
1 cup	no-fat yogurt	250 mL
1 tbsp.	maple syrup	15 mL
	Raspberry Sauce (page 17)	
	Mint leaves for garnish	

1. Combine water, sugar, lemon zest and juice and vanilla in a large saucepan; bring to a boil.
2. Add peeled pears. Make sure they are covered with liquid; add more water if needed.
3. Reduce heat to medium low and simmer for 15 minutes.
4. Remove pan from heat and cool pears in liquid. Then drain well on paper towels.
5. Combine the yogurt and maple syrup.
6. To serve, put a dollop of yogurt on each plate. Place the pear in the centre of the yogurt. Drizzle Raspberry Sauce down the side of the pear. Decorate the stem with a mint leaf.

Preparation Note

The pears can be cooked a day ahead of time and kept in their liquid in the fridge until ready to serve.

Raspberry Sauce

½ cup	water	125 mL
½ cup	sugar	125 mL
4 cups	raspberries	1 L
1 tbsp.	lemon juice	15 mL
1 tbsp.	kirsch (optional)	15 mL

1. Combine water and sugar in a saucepan; bring to a boil. Remove pan from heat.
2. Blend raspberries until smooth; add to the sugar syrup.
3. Stir in lemon juice, and kirsch if desired. Cool.

Preparation Note

Unsweetened frozen berries can be used, but reduce water to ¼ cup (50 mL).

Spring Fling

FOR 4

Mushroom Tomato Bouillon

(Fresh Rolls)

Chicken Parmesan

(Pasta)

Green Beans and Almonds

Fruit Bounty

Mushroom Tomato Bouillon

SERVES 4

~~~~~~~~~~~~~~~~~~~~~

1 can (19 oz.)	whole tomatoes	1 can (540 mL)
1 can (10 oz.)	consommé	1 can (284 mL)
1 cup	water	250 mL
1	clove garlic, minced	1
1 cup	sliced mushrooms	250 mL
¼ cup	sherry	50 mL
	Parsley for garnish	

1. Place tomatoes in a large saucepan. Crush with a hand blender.
2. Over medium heat add consommé, water and garlic. Stir well to blend.
3. Add mushrooms; simmer for about 10 minutes.
4. Remove from heat. Stir in sherry.
5. Ladle into bowls. Garnish with parsley.

Chicken Parmesan

SERVES 4

Oven: 400°F/200°C

1 tsp.	olive oil	5 mL
1	onion, chopped	1
1	clove garlic, minced	1
1 can (28 oz.)	tomatoes, blended	1 can (796 mL)
	Salt and pepper to taste	
1 tsp.	dried basil	5 mL
½ cup	crushed cornflakes	125 mL
¼ cup	low-fat Parmesan cheese	50 mL
5 or 6	boneless, skinless chicken breasts	5 or 6
2	egg whites, beaten until frothy	2
¾ cup	shredded low-fat mozzarella cheese	175 mL

1. Heat oil in a medium, heavy saucepan. Sauté onion and garlic until onion is softened.
2. Add blended tomatoes, salt, pepper and basil. Bring to a boil and simmer for 5 minutes. Remove from heat.
3. In a shallow dish, combine cornflake crumbs and Parmesan cheese.

4. Dip chicken breasts into the egg whites and then dredge in the cornflake crumbs.
5. Place chicken in a casserole dish coated with cooking spray. Bake 30 minutes. Meanwhile, reheat tomato sauce.
6. Remove chicken from oven. Pour tomato sauce over it. Top with mozzarella. Bake 15 minutes more or until chicken is cooked through.
7. Serve with your favourite pasta.

Preparation Note

Try substituting Veggie Slices for mozzarella cheese.

Green Beans and Almonds

~~~~~~~~~~~~~~~~~~~~

1 lb.	fresh green beans	500 g
1 tsp.	light butter	5 mL
1 cup	sliced mushrooms	250 mL
¼ cup	toasted slivered almonds	50 mL

1. Bring beans to a boil and simmer for 3 or 4 minutes or until tender but still crisp. Drain.
2. Melt butter in a frying pan over medium-high heat. Sauté the mushrooms until tender.
3. Add the drained beans. Stir until well mixed and beans are heated through.
4. Place in serving dish. Top with toasted almonds.

Fruit Bounty

~~~~~~

1	red apple, diced	1
1	pear, diced	1
1	orange, sectioned	1
2	bananas, sliced	2
1 cup	halved seedless grapes	250 mL
½	cantaloupe, diced	½
2	kiwis, sliced	2
1 cup	sliced strawberries	250 mL
1 cup	orange juice	250 mL

1. Place prepared fruit in a large bowl, toss with orange juice and chill.

Serving Suggestion

For extra flavour, add ¼ cup (50 mL) Grand Marnier to the orange juice.

Four Ladies and a Lunch

FOR 4

Minted Iced Tea

Greek Salad

Falafel

Lemon Loaf

Frozen Green Grapes

Minted Iced Tea

~~~~~~~~~~~~~~~~~~~~~~~~~~~~~~~~~~

Mint leaves
Ice cubes
1 pot black tea, cooled
Sugar
Mint sprigs for garnish

1. Crush several mint leaves against the side of each glass.
2. Fill glasses with ice cubes and fill with tea.
3. Sweeten with sugar to taste. Garnish each glass with a sprig of mint.

Greek Salad

~~~~~~~~~~~~~~~~~~~~~~~~~~~~~~~~

2	large tomatoes, cut into chunks	2
1	cucumber, cut into chunks	1
1	green pepper, cut into chunks	1
1	red onion, cut into chunks	1
12	Kalamata olives	12
1 cup	crumbled low-fat feta cheese	250 mL
2 tbsp.	dried oregano	30 mL
3 tbsp.	lemon juice	45 mL
1 tbsp.	olive oil	15 mL

1. In a shallow bowl or on a platter, combine all ingredients. Toss gently to mix.
2. Serve at room temperature.

Falafel

~~~~~~~~~~~~~~~~~~~~~~~~~~~~~~~~~~~~

1 can (19 oz.)	chickpeas, rinsed and drained	1 can (540 mL)
2	onions, chopped	2
⅓ cup	dried bread crumbs	75 mL
2 tbsp.	chopped fresh parsley	30 mL
2 tbsp.	ground cumin	30 mL
2	cloves garlic, minced	2
1 tsp.	pepper	5 mL
¼ tsp.	salt	1 mL
4	pita breads	4
2 cups	shredded lettuce	500 mL
1	tomato, chopped	1
	Tzatziki Sauce (page 28)	

1. Combine chickpeas, half of the onions, bread crumbs and seasonings in a food processor. Whirl until well blended.
2. Divide mixture into 12 equal portions. Roll each into a ball and flatten slightly.
3. Coat a nonstick skillet with cooking spray. Heat over medium heat; add falafel balls. Cook 2 or 3 minutes per side or until lightly browned.
4. Cut each pita in half. Place some lettuce and 3 falafel balls inside each pocket.
5. Garnish with tomato and remaining onion. Top with Tzatziki Sauce.

Tzatziki Sauce

Yields 2 cups/500 mL

1 cup	no-fat plain yogurt	250 mL
¼ cup	tahini or low-fat peanut butter	50 mL
3 tbsp.	lemon juice	45 mL
1	clove garlic, crushed	1
¼ tsp.	salt	1 mL
¼ tsp.	pepper	1 mL
½	cucumber, peeled and thinly sliced	½

1. Place all ingredients except the cucumber in a food processor and whirl until smooth.
2. Stir in cucumber. Chill.

Lemon Loaf

~~~~~~~~~~~~~~~~~~~~~~~~~~~~~~~~

Oven: 350°F/180°C

¼ cup	light butter	50 mL
¾ cup	sugar	175 mL
1	egg	1
1	egg white	1
	Grated zest of 1 lemon	
2 cups	all-purpose flour	500 mL
4 tsp.	baking powder	20 mL
	Pinch salt	
¾ cup	skim milk	175 mL
3 tbsp.	lemon juice	45 mL
2 tbsp.	sugar	30 mL

1. Cream butter and sugar in mixing bowl.
2. Beat in egg and egg white.
3. Stir in lemon zest.
4. Combine flour, baking powder and salt in a bowl; beat into creamed mixture, alternating with the milk.
5. Pour into a 9- x 5-inch (2 L) loaf pan coated with cooking spray. Bake for 50 minutes or until tester comes out clean.
6. Combine the lemon juice and sugar. Pour the glaze over the loaf. Return loaf to the oven for 5 more minutes.
7. Turn loaf out onto a rack. When loaf is cool, wrap and store for a day before serving.

Frozen Green Grapes

SERVES 4

~~~~~~~~~~~~~~~~

| 1 | large bunch green grapes | 1 |

1. Remove grapes from stems. Place on a baking sheet and freeze.
2. Serve in a glass bowl.

Preparation Note

These are a very popular snack with kids!

Chili on the Run

FOR 4

Quick Chili Chowder

Corn Bread

Bananas with Rhubarb Sauce

Quick Chili Chowder

~~~~~~~~~~~~~~~~~~~~~~~

1 tbsp.	olive oil	15 mL
1	large onion, chopped	1
1	green pepper, chopped	1
1 can (28 oz.)	tomatoes, chopped	1 can (796 mL)
1 cup	vegetable broth	250 mL
1 tsp.	Mexican chili powder	5 mL
1 can (14 oz.)	kidney beans	1 can (398 mL)
1 can (14 oz.)	kernel corn	1 can (398 mL)

1. In a large, heavy skillet, heat oil; sauté onion and pepper until tender.
2. Add tomatoes, broth and chili powder. Simmer over medium heat for 15 minutes.
3. Add kidney beans and corn. Simmer 10 minutes longer, stirring occasionally.

Corn Bread

Oven: 425°F/220°C

1	egg	1
1 cup	no-fat sour cream	250 mL
¼ cup	skim milk	50 mL
1 cup	cornmeal	250 mL
1 cup	all-purpose flour	250 mL
3 tbsp.	brown sugar	45 mL
1 tsp.	baking powder	5 mL
1 tsp.	cream of tartar	5 mL
¾ tsp.	salt	4 mL
2 tbsp.	applesauce	30 mL

1. In a large bowl beat together the egg, sour cream and milk.
2. In another bowl, combine all the dry ingredients. Slowly stir them into the egg mixture; stir only until combined.
3. Slowly stir in applesauce.
4. Spray a 9- x 5-inch (2 L) loaf pan with cooking spray and pour mixture into pan.
5. Bake 20 minutes or until golden brown and a knife inserted in centre comes out clean.

Bananas with Rhubarb Sauce

SERVES 4

1 lb.	rhubarb, cut in 1-inch (2.5 cm) pieces	500 g
¼ cup	orange juice	50 mL
¼ cup	water	50 mL
¾ cup	sugar (or to taste)	175 mL
½ tsp.	cinnamon	2 mL
4	bananas	4
½ cup	toasted slivered almonds	125 mL

1. In a medium saucepan, combine rhubarb, orange juice, water, sugar and cinnamon. Cook over medium heat, stirring occasionally, until rhubarb begins to fall apart and thicken. Remove from heat.
2. Peel bananas, cut in half and slice lengthwise.
3. Place a banana on each plate. Top with rhubarb sauce and toasted almonds.

Rise and Shine Brunch

FOR 4

Orange Smoothy

Mushroom Frittata

(Whole-Wheat Toast)

Fresh Fruit Mosaic

Banana Bread

Orange Smoothy

S E R V E S 4

~~~~~~~~~~~~~~~~~~~~~~~~~

4 cups	cold orange juice	1 L
3	bananas	3

1. Place juice and bananas in a blender. Process until smooth. (A hand blender can also be used.)

Preparation Note

Add 6 large strawberries when they are in season.

Mushroom Frittata

SERVES 4

~~~~~~

2 tsp.	olive oil	10 mL
2	cloves garlic, finely chopped	2
½ cup	chopped onions	125 mL
2 cups	sliced mushrooms	500 mL
¼ cup	chopped fresh parsley	50 mL
10	egg whites	10
	Salt and pepper to taste	

1. Heat oil in a large nonstick skillet over medium-high heat. Add garlic and onions. Sauté for 2 minutes.
2. Add mushrooms; cook, stirring, for 2 more minutes.
3. Reduce heat to medium. Stir in parsley.
4. Pour egg whites over vegetable mixture.
5. Stir in salt and pepper to taste. Cover and cook for 5 minutes or until eggs are set. Serve immediately.

Serving Suggestion

Serve with whole-wheat toast. To make a complete protein, you must have a whole grain with any nonmeat protein.

Fresh Fruit Mosaic

1 cup	halved seedless grapes	250 mL
2 cups	halved strawberries	500 mL
2	oranges, sectioned	2
1	small melon, cubed	1
1	grapefruit, sectioned, and sections halved	1
1	apple, cubed	1
1	pear, cubed	1
1	banana, sliced	1
¼ cup	freshly squeezed lemon juice	50 mL

1. Combine all fresh fruit and drizzle with lemon juice. Toss. Chill for at least 1 hour before serving.

Banana Bread

~~~~~~~~~~~~~~~~~~~~~~~~~~~~

Oven: 350°F/180°C

1	egg	1
½ cup	sugar	125 mL
2 tbsp.	canola oil	30 mL
3	bananas, mashed	3
2 tbsp.	sweetened applesauce	30 mL
1½ cups	all-purpose flour	375 mL
1 tsp.	baking powder	5 mL
1 tsp.	baking soda	5 mL
1 tsp.	grated lemon zest	5 mL

1. Beat egg, sugar and oil together in a mixing bowl or food processor.
2. Add mashed bananas and applesauce.
3. Combine the dry ingredients and lemon zest. Stir into the banana mixture.
4. Pour into a lightly greased nonstick 9- x 5-inch (2 L) loaf pan. Bake for 1 hour or until tester comes out clean. Let stand for 10 minutes, then turn out onto a rack.

Opening Up the Cottage

FOR 6

Bruschetta

Traditional Veggie Lasagna

Lemon Broccoli Salad

Strawberry-Rhubarb Tango

Bruschetta

~~~~~~~~~~~~~~~~~~~~~~~~~~~~~~~

1 tbsp.	olive oil	15 mL
1	clove garlic, crushed	1
2	medium tomatoes, diced	2
1 tbsp.	dried basil (or 2 tbsp./30 mL chopped fresh)	15 mL
1	baguette	1
½ cup	crumbled feta cheese	125 mL

1. Combine oil, garlic, tomatoes and basil. Let stand for about 20 minutes.
2. Slice baguette into 1-inch (2.5 cm) slices.
3. Spread tomato mixture over slices. Sprinkle with crumbled feta cheese.
4. Place under broiler until lightly browned.
5. Serve immediately.

Traditional Veggie Lasagna

~~~~~~~~~~~~~~~~~~~~~~~~~~~~~~

Oven: 350°F/180°C

1 tsp.	olive oil	5 mL
1	medium onion, chopped	1
2	cloves garlic, minced	2
2 cups	sliced mushrooms	500 mL
1 cup	chopped celery	250 mL
1 cup	sliced carrots	250 mL
½ cup	chopped green pepper	125 mL
1 can (28 oz.)	chopped tomatoes	1 can (796 mL)
1 tsp.	dried oregano	5 mL
1 tsp.	dried basil	5 mL
¼ tsp.	dried chili flakes (optional)	1 mL
	Salt and pepper to taste	
9–12	lasagna noodles	9–12
2 cups	low-fat cottage cheese	500 mL
2 cups	shredded low-fat mozzarella cheese	500 mL

1. In a nonstick frying pan, heat oil; sauté onions until tender.
2. Add garlic, mushrooms, celery, carrots and green pepper. Stir-fry for 5 minutes.

3. Transfer the vegetables to a medium saucepan. Add tomatoes, oregano, basil, chili flakes (if desired), salt and pepper. Bring to a boil, reduce heat to medium, and cook for 20 minutes, stirring occasionally.

4. Meanwhile, cook the lasagna noodles and drain.

5. In a 13- x 9-inch (3.5 L) baking pan, arrange a layer of noodles. Top with half of the sauce and half of the cottage cheese. Repeat layers, ending with noodles. Top with mozzarella cheese. Bake for 45 minutes or until bubbling. Let stand for 10 minutes before serving.

Lemon Broccoli Salad

~~~~~~~~~~~~~~~~~~

2½ lb.	broccoli florets	1.25 kg
1	red pepper, thinly sliced	1
4	stalks celery, cut in ½-inch (1 cm) pieces	4
¼ cup	olive oil	50 mL
4 tbsp.	fresh lemon juice	60 mL
	Salt and freshly ground pepper to taste	

1. Cook broccoli florets in boiling salted water for 4 to 5 minutes or until tender but still crisp. Drain and cool.
2. Place broccoli in a salad bowl; add red pepper slices and celery pieces.
3. Combine olive oil, lemon juice, salt and pepper. Drizzle over salad mixture. Toss.
4. Serve immediately.

Strawberry-Rhubarb Tango

SERVES 6

5 cups	fresh rhubarb cut in 1-inch (2.5 cm) pieces	1.25 L
2 cups	strawberries	500 mL
1½ cups	water	375 mL
1 cup	sugar (or to taste)	250 mL

1. Combine rhubarb, strawberries and water in a saucepan. Bring to a boil. Reduce heat and simmer for 15 minutes or until fruit is completely cooked.
2. Add sugar and stir until well combined. Remove from heat.
3. Serve warm or cold.

Victoria Day Blast

FOR 6

Orange-Ginger Chicken

(White Rice)

Tossed Salad with Raspberry Vinaigrette

Citrus Tiramisu

Orange-Ginger Chicken

SERVES 6

1 tsp.	sesame oil	5 mL
½ tsp.	chili oil	2 mL
6	boneless, skinless chicken breasts	6
½ cup	orange marmalade	125 mL
3 tbsp.	low-sodium soy sauce	45 mL
1 tbsp.	grated fresh ginger	15 mL
1 tbsp.	water	15 mL
2	cloves garlic, minced	2

1. Heat oils in a nonstick skillet over medium heat.
2. Add chicken; cook 6 minutes on each side or until chicken is done.
3. Meanwhile, combine remaining ingredients. Pour mixture over chicken, and continue to stir and baste for 2 minutes.
4. Remove from heat and serve immediately with white rice.

Serving Suggestion

Instead of white rice, serve with **Rice Pilaf** (see page 81) if preferred.

Tossed Salad with Raspberry Vinaigrette

1	head romaine	1
2 cups	sliced mushrooms	500 mL
½ cup	sliced radishes	125 mL
1	small red onion, sliced	1
	Raspberry Vinaigrette (below)	

1. Toss lettuce and vegetables with Raspberry Vinaigrette just before serving.

Raspberry Vinaigrette

Yields ⅓ cup/75 mL

2 tbsp.	olive oil	30 mL
2 tbsp.	raspberry vinegar	30 mL
1½ tsp.	sugar	7 mL
	Pinch salt	
¼ tsp.	dry mustard	1 mL
1	clove garlic, minced	1

1. Combine all ingredients in a jar and shake well.

Preparation Note

Red wine vinegar or balsamic vinegar can be used instead of raspberry vinegar.

Citrus Tiramisu

SERVES 6

~~~~~~~~~~~~~~~~~~~~~~~~~~~~~~~~

8 oz.	light cream cheese	250 g
4 oz.	mascarpone cheese	125 g
¼ cup	sugar	50 mL
2 tbsp.	cognac	30 mL
1½ cups	hot water	375 mL
2 tbsp.	instant espresso coffee	30 mL
24	ladyfingers	24
1 cup	chopped orange sections	250 mL
1 tbsp.	cocoa	15 mL
¼ cup	candied mixed peel	50 mL

1. In a food processor, process the cream cheese, mascarpone cheese, sugar and cognac until smooth. Set aside.
2. Combine hot water and coffee in a small bowl. Stir well.
3. Split ladyfingers in half lengthwise.
4. Quickly dip ladyfinger halves, flat side down, into the coffee. Arrange dipped side down in an 8- x 8-inch (2 L) square baking dish.
5. Spread half of the cheese mixture evenly over the ladyfingers. Top with half of the oranges.
6. Repeat with the remaining ladyfinger halves, coffee and cream cheese mixture. Top with remaining oranges.
7. Cover with plastic wrap and chill for at least 8 hours.
8. To serve, sprinkle with cocoa and top with candied peel.

Spring Fry

FOR 4

Peppery Beef Stir-Fry

(White Rice)

Honey-Sesame Asparagus

Tangy Orange Mousse

Peppery Beef Stir-Fry

SERVES 4

~~~~~~~~~~~~~~~~~~~~~~~~~~~~~~

½ lb.	tender steak	250 g
2 tbsp.	soy sauce	30 mL
2 tsp.	sugar	10 mL
2 tsp.	grated fresh ginger	10 mL
½ tsp.	sesame oil	2 mL
1 tbsp.	olive oil	15 mL
1	clove garlic, minced	1
2	small onions, quartered	2
1	small red pepper, cut in strips	1
1–2 tsp.	crushed black pepper	5–10 mL
1¼ cups	water	300 mL
1 tbsp.	cornstarch	15 mL

1. Cut beef across the grain into thin strips.
2. Combine the soy sauce, sugar, ginger and sesame oil. In a shallow dish or resealable plastic bag, combine beef and marinade. Marinate for about 30 minutes, stirring occasionally.
3. Heat oil in a large, heavy skillet or wok over high heat. Stir-fry garlic and beef for several minutes.
4. Add onions, red pepper and black pepper. Stir-fry several more minutes or until vegetables are slightly tender.
5. Combine water and cornstarch. Add to pan. Bring mixture to a boil and cook, stirring, until thickened. If gravy is too thick, add more water.
6. Serve over white rice.

Honey-Sesame Asparagus

SERVES 4

~~~~~~~~~~~~~~~~~~~~~~~~~~~~~~~~

½ lb.	asparagus	250 g
1 tsp.	sesame oil	5 mL
1 tsp.	sesame seeds	5 mL
1½ cups	snow peas	375 mL
2 tsp.	honey	10 mL
¼ tsp.	grated fresh ginger	1 mL
	Salt to taste	

1. Cut asparagus spears into thirds. Steam until slightly tender, about 3 minutes.
2. Heat sesame oil in a heavy skillet or wok over high heat. Add sesame seeds and snow peas; stir-fry about 2 minutes.
3. Add asparagus, honey, ginger and salt. Cook, stirring, several more minutes until piping hot.
4. Serve immediately.

Preparation Note

Green beans can be substituted for the asparagus.

Tangy Orange Mousse

~~~~~~~~~~~~~~~~~~~~~~~~~~~~~~

1 cup	orange juice	250 mL
⅓ cup	sugar	75 mL
3 tsp.	gelatine (1 package)	15 mL
¼ cup	dry white wine	50 mL
1 cup	no-fat yogurt	250 mL
3 tbsp.	brown sugar	45 mL
4	orange slices	4

1. Combine orange juice, sugar and gelatine in a saucepan. Stir over medium heat until sugar and gelatine are dissolved; do not let boil.
2. Remove from heat and stir in wine.
3. Chill in the refrigerator or freezer for approximately 20 minutes until mousse has set to the consistency of unbeaten egg white.
4. Combine yogurt and brown sugar, stirring vigorously to dissolve sugar.
5. Fold yogurt into the thickened orange mixture.
6. Pour into individual stemmed glasses and chill.
7. Garnish with a twisted orange slice when ready to serve.

Preparation Note

Can be prepared a day ahead.

2

Summer

~~~~~~~~~~

A SUMMER ON GEORGIAN BAY is quite simply an experience in life that stirs the soul. Authors have written books about it. Songwriters have put music to it. Photographers have captured it on film. But we are the lucky ones, because we live it, and our families have the memories of all those wonderful summers by the Bay.

When our children were younger they would go to day camp at the Wye Marsh or listen to the stories of the Jesuits and the Ouendat peoples at Saint Marie Among the Hurons. They would make sandcastles on the beach at Beckwith, and learn how to build a canoe at Camp Kitchikewana on Beausoleil Island. Now that they are older, they have had summer jobs as interpreters at the historic sites, counsellors at the island camps, dock-hands at the busy marinas or rangers at any one of the nearby national or provincial parks. Anything to spend the summer on Georgian Bay before going back to university in the fall or starting a new job.

Our older children are taking part in the rites of summer as we did in our younger days. Dock-launching day is a command performance, and you are finally old enough to have a beer with Dad when it's all done. Now that you have passed the Canadian Power Squadron Course, you can take the boat up to Sans Souci. You have to be able to tell the story that you swam to the red can and back (during a three-day blow). And you very definitely must have jumped off Elephant Rock into McCrea Lake on or before your nineteenth birthday! Oh, the days of summer are never lost . . .

In cottage country it often happens that unexpected company floats up to your dock or strolls onto your beach on one of those glorious summer afternoons. You can be well prepared for these occasions if you have a good barbecue and a fairly large freezer. And if you make sure to keep plenty of seasonal local fresh fruits and vegetables on hand, unexpected entertaining can be a summer breeze.

Now that we have a few more summers under our belts, the large slabs of meat on the barbie are more often replaced by grilled chicken, fish, and lots of vegetables. Check out our Down by the Bay menu, with its Aromatic Curried Shrimp, or try our Summer Salmon Sizzle for a different method of cooking fish on the barbecue. And for a special treat, our Elegant Lamb really is an elegant menu, with summer simplicity in mind.

Picture this: it's the long weekend, all the kids have a day off, and all their friends have come to visit from the other beaches. The big strapping guys spend the afternoon waterskiing in front of the sun-worshipping girls on the dock. We enjoy watching all the fun from our lawnchairs. As the warm summer sun starts to dip behind the Giant's Tomb, they are all hungry—really, really hungry! Fortunately our kids are part of today's health-conscious generation, so our Kick-Start Summer BBQ will be the perfect crowd-pleaser.

Later on, it's your time with your favourite summer chum. Hop into the boat, cruise on out into the open bay and enjoy together the last moments of that incredible Georgian Bay sunset. Take along some nibbles from our Party Time section, and you are sure to enjoy the finest show of the season.

Kick-Start Summer BBQ

FOR 8

Zippy Nachos

Asparagus with Creamy Dipping Sauce

Sassy Chicken Burgers

Santa Fe Potato Salad

Corny Summer Salad

Black Bean Salad

Gingered Melon Mix

Zippy Nachos

~~~~~~~~~~~~~~~~~~~~~~~~

1 bag (12 oz.)	nacho chips	1 bag (375 g)
3	large tomatoes, diced	3
1	green pepper, diced	1
1	small onion, diced	1
	Cayenne pepper (optional)	
2 cups	shredded light mozzarella cheese	500 mL

1. Place nachos on a large tray or ovenproof platter.
2. Arrange tomatoes, green pepper and onion over the nachos.
3. Sprinkle with cayenne pepper for a bit of a zip.
4. Top with mozzarella. Place under broiler for several minutes until cheese is melted.

Preparation Note

This recipe can also be heated in the microwave. Divide into 2 batches, and use a microwave-safe platter. Heat on High for 1 to 2 minutes.

Asparagus with Creamy Dipping Sauce

SERVES 8

~~~~~~~~~~~~~~~~~~~~~~~~~~

3 lb.	pencil-thin asparagus	1.5 kg
	Creamy Dipping Sauce (below)	

1. Wash and trim asparagus.
2. Arrange asparagus on serving dish and serve with sauce.

Creamy Dipping Sauce

Yields 2¼ cups/550 mL

8 oz.	light cream cheese, softened	250 g
1 cup	no-fat sour cream	250 mL
3	green onions, minced	3
3 tbsp.	drained capers	45 mL
2 tbsp.	chopped fresh parsley	30 mL
1 tbsp.	chopped fresh dill	15 mL
2 tbsp.	Dijon mustard	30 mL
	Pinch each tarragon, basil and marjoram	
	Salt and pepper to taste	

(continued)

1. Combine all ingredients in a mixing bowl and blend until smooth. Cover and chill until ready to serve.

Preparation Note

Sauce can be made up to 3 days ahead and stored in the refrigerator.

Sassy Chicken Burgers

SERVES 8

~~~~~~~~~~~~~~~~~~~~~~~~~~

2 lb.	ground chicken or turkey	1 kg.
4 tbsp.	low-fat mayonnaise	60 mL
2	egg whites	2
½ cup	finely chopped celery	125 mL
½ cup	finely chopped green onions	125 mL
2 tsp.	dried dillweed	10 mL
	Salt and pepper to taste	
8	focaccia buns	8
4	tomatoes, chopped	4
4 cups	shredded lettuce	1 L
	Herbed Burg Sauce (page 64)	

1. In a large bowl, combine chicken, mayonnaise, egg whites, celery, green onions, dill, salt and pepper. Shape into 8 patties.
2. Grill patties on barbecue over medium heat 4 minutes per side or until no longer pink inside.
3. Place each patty on one bun; sprinkle with tomatoes and lettuce. Add a dollop of Herbed Burg Sauce.
4. Serve immediately.

Herbed Burg Sauce

Yields 1 cup/250 mL

½ cup	low-fat mayonnaise	125 mL
½ cup	no-fat sour cream	125 mL
2 tbsp.	chopped fresh parsley	30 mL
2	cloves garlic, minced	2
	Freshly ground pepper to taste	

1. Combine all ingredients. Chill until ready to serve.

Santa Fe Potato Salad

SERVES 8 TO 10

~~~~~~~~~~~~~~~~~~~~~~~~

10	large potatoes, peeled	10
4	stalks celery, finely chopped	4
2	green peppers, chopped	2
⅔ cup	sliced green olives	150 mL
6	green onions, chopped	6
2 cups	medium-hot salsa	500 mL
1 cup	low-fat sour cream	250 mL
½ cup	low-fat mayonnaise	125 mL
	Salt and pepper to taste	

1. Boil potatoes until just cooked and still firm. Drain and cool. Cut into small cubes. Place in a large bowl.
2. Add celery, green peppers, olives and green onions. Gently mix.
3. Combine salsa, sour cream and mayonnaise. Fold into vegetables and gently mix.
4. Add salt and pepper to taste.
5. Cover and chill until serving time.

Preparation Note

For fresh salsa, see Salsa Dip, page 123.

Corny Summer Salad

4 cups	corn kernels	1 L
2 cups	diced mushrooms	500 mL
2 cups	diced green onions	500 mL
2 tbsp.	olive oil	30 mL
2 tbsp.	lemon juice	30 mL
1 tbsp.	chopped fresh dill	15 mL
1 tbsp.	chopped fresh basil	15 mL
1 tbsp.	Worcestershire sauce	15 mL
1 tsp.	paprika	5 mL
½ tsp.	salt	2 mL
4	cloves garlic, minced	4

1. Combine all ingredients.
2. Let salad stand for several hours or overnight before serving.

Black Bean Salad

~~~~~~

4 tbsp.	minced fresh coriander	60 mL
2 tbsp.	chopped fresh parsley	30 mL
2 tbsp.	fresh lime juice	30 mL
½ tsp.	salt	2 mL
½ tsp.	pepper	2 mL
2 cans (14 oz.)	black beans, rinsed and drained	2 cans (398 mL)
2	avocados, diced	2
½ cup	chopped green onions	125 mL
8 cups	mixed salad greens	2 L

1. Whisk together coriander, parsley, lime juice, salt and pepper.
2. Add beans, avocados and green onions. Cover and chill for 2 hours.
3. Serve over salad greens.

Gingered Melon Mix

~~~~~~~~~~~~~~~~~~~~~

¼ cup	liquid honey	50 mL
¼ cup	water	50 mL
2 tsp.	grated lime zest	10 mL
6 tbsp.	fresh lime juice	90 mL
2 tbsp.	chopped peeled fresh ginger	30 mL
2 tbsp.	chopped fresh mint	30 mL
8 cups	1-inch (2.5-cm) watermelon balls	2 L
2 cups	1-inch (2.5-cm) honeydew melon balls	500 mL
2 cups	1-inch (2.5-cm) cantaloupe balls	500 mL
	Mint sprigs for garnish	

1. In a small bowl, whisk together honey, water, lime zest, lime juice, ginger and mint. Set aside.
2. Combine melon balls in a large serving bowl. Toss with lime juice mixture. Cover and chill at least 1 hour.
3. Garnish with mint sprigs before serving.

Down by the Bay . . .

FOR 4

Aromatic Curried Shrimp

(Rice)

Spinach and Watermelon Salad

*Cantaloupe and Blackberries
with Almond Cream*

Aromatic Curried Shrimp

~~~~~~~~~~~~~~~~~~~~~~~~~~~~~~~~~

1½ lb.	large shrimp, peeled and deveined	750 g
1 tbsp.	all-purpose flour	15 mL
2 tsp.	vegetable oil	10 mL
½ cup	chopped green onions	125 mL
1 tbsp.	curry powder	15 mL
1 cup	diced red pepper	250 mL
1½ cups	diced tomato	375 mL
½ cup	light coconut milk	125 mL
¼ cup	chopped fresh basil	50 mL
	(or 3 tsp./15 mL dried)	
1 tbsp.	lemon juice	15 mL
1 tsp.	sugar	5 mL
1 cup	low-fat chicken broth	250 mL
	Flaked sweetened coconut for garnish	

1. In a bowl, toss shrimp with flour until coated. Set aside.
2. Heat oil in a large skillet or wok over medium heat.
3. Sauté onions and curry powder 2 or 3 minutes.
4. Add red pepper and sauté 1 minute.
5. Add tomato, coconut milk, basil, lemon juice, sugar and broth. Bring to a boil. Reduce heat and simmer 2 to 3 minutes, stirring occasionally.
6. Add shrimp and simmer, stirring occasionally, for 4 minutes or until shrimp are just cooked.
7. To serve, spoon shrimp mixture over cooked rice and garnish with coconut.

Spinach and Watermelon Salad

~~~~~~~~~~~~~~~~~~~~~~~~~~~~~~~~~

1 tbsp.	honey	15 mL
1 tbsp.	balsamic vinegar	15 mL
1 tbsp.	water	15 mL
1½ tsp.	olive oil	7 mL
½ tsp.	lemon juice	2 mL
½ tsp.	dried tarragon	2 mL
	Salt and pepper to taste	
4 cups	torn spinach leaves	1 L
4 cups	torn romaine	1 L
2 cups	watermelon balls	500 mL
1 cup	sliced strawberries	250 mL
½ cup	sliced cucumber	125 mL
¼ cup	thinly sliced red onion	50 mL

1. In a bowl or jar combine honey, vinegar, water, olive oil, lemon juice, salt and pepper; mix well. Set aside.
2. Combine spinach and romaine with the remaining ingredients in a large bowl.
3. Drizzle dressing over salad and toss.

Cantaloupe and Blackberries with Almond Cream

SERVES 4

Yields 1 cup/250 mL

4 oz.	light cream cheese, softened	125 g
4 oz.	almond tofu	125 g
1 tbsp.	maple syrup	15 mL
1	cantaloupe, peeled and seeded	1
1 cup	blackberries	250 mL
¼ cup	toasted sliced almonds	50 mL
	Mint sprigs for garnish	

1. In a food processor or blender, blend cream cheese, almond tofu and syrup until smooth. Pour into a small bowl and set aside.
2. Cut cantaloupe lengthwise into ¼-inch (5 mm) slices. On individual serving plates, arrange slices of cantaloupe. Top each serving with blackberries and a dollop of the cream cheese mixture.
3. Sprinkle with toasted almonds and garnish with mint sprigs.

Preparation Note

Any berry can be substituted for the blackberries.

Serving Suggestion

Use the almond cream as a dip for fruit.

My Thai

FOR 8

Thai Noodles

Oriental Pork Grill

Broccoli-Raisin Salad

Citrus-Cucumber Salad

Tropical Fruit Cocktail

Thai Noodles

~~~~~~~~~~~~~~~~~~~~~~

¼ cup	olive oil	50 mL
1–2 tsp.	sesame oil	5–10 mL
⅓ cup	soy sauce	75 mL
¼ cup	rice vinegar	50 mL
2 tbsp.	sugar	30 mL
1 or 2	small red hot chili peppers, minced	1 or 2
2 tbsp.	grated fresh ginger	30 mL
6	cloves garlic, minced	6
	Black pepper to taste	
1 lb.	spaghetti	500 g
1	large tomato, diced	1
1	green pepper, diced	1
4	green onions, sliced	4
¼ cup	chopped fresh coriander for garnish	50 mL

1. Place oils, soy sauce, vinegar, sugar, chili peppers, ginger, garlic and black pepper in a jar; shake well. Refrigerate.
2. Cook spaghetti. Rinse under cold water and drain.
3. In a large bowl, pour dressing over the spaghetti. Add the tomato, green pepper and green onions. Toss. Refrigerate until chilled, tossing several times to mix the flavours.
4. Serve in a large bowl or on a platter, garnished with fresh coriander.

Preparation Note

Make up the spaghetti with the dressing the day before. Let stand overnight to enhance the flavour. Toss several times. Garnish just before serving.

Oriental Pork Grill

SERVES 8

~~~~~~~~~~~~~~~~~~~~~

8	large pork chops	8
2 tbsp.	olive oil	30 mL
½ cup	soy sauce	125 mL
¼ cup	chopped fresh coriander	50 mL
¼ cup	sherry	50 mL
3 tbsp.	honey	45 mL
2 tbsp.	grated fresh ginger	30 mL
2 tbsp.	lime juice	30 mL
3	cloves garlic, minced	3
2	green onions, sliced	2

1. Trim fat from pork chops. Place chops in a flat container.
2. Combine remaining ingredients in a jar and shake well.
3. Pour over the pork chops and marinate, covered and refrigerated, 6 to 8 hours, turning periodically.
4. Cook on barbecue over medium heat, basting occasionally with the marinade.

Broccoli-Raisin Salad

~~~~~~~~~~~~~~~~~~~~~~~~~~~~

2	bunches broccoli, cooked or raw	2
1 cup	finely chopped onion	250 mL
1 cup	raisins	250 mL
½ cup	sunflower seeds	125 mL
½ cup	no-fat mayonnaise	125 mL
3 tbsp.	white vinegar	45 mL
1 tbsp.	sugar	15 mL
	Salt and pepper to taste	

1. Cut the broccoli, including the stems, into bite-sized pieces.
2. In a large bowl, combine the broccoli, onion, raisins and sunflower seeds.
3. In a separate bowl, whisk together the mayonnaise, vinegar and sugar. Season with salt and pepper.
4. Pour the dressing over the broccoli mixture and mix well. Chill.

Citrus-Cucumber Salad

~~~~~~~~~~~~~~~~~~~~~~~~~~~~~~~~~~~~~

1	large seedless cucumber, sliced	1
2 cans (10 oz.)	mandarin orange segments, drained	2 cans (284 mL)
½ cup	sliced radishes	125 mL
2 tbsp.	olive oil	30 mL
2 tbsp.	lemon juice	30 mL
¼ tsp.	salt	1 mL
	Fresh parsley sprigs for garnish	

1. In a bowl, toss together cucumber slices, orange segments and radishes.
2. In a measuring cup or small bowl, mix the oil, lemon juice and salt. Drizzle over cucumber mixture.
3. Garnish with fresh parsley.

Tropical Fruit Cocktail

SERVES 8

~~~~~~~~~~~~~~~~

1	honeydew melon, peeled and cubed	1
1	fresh pineapple, peeled and cubed	1
2	fresh mangoes, peeled and cubed	2
	Lime Rum Sauce (below)	

1. Place fruit in a shallow bowl.
2. Prepare Lime Rum Sauce and pour over fruit. Chill, covered, for several hours, stirring occasionally.

Lime Rum Sauce

Yields 1½ cups/375 mL

⅔ cup	sugar	150 mL
⅓ cup	water	75 mL
1 tsp.	grated lime zest	5 mL
6 tbsp.	lime juice	90 mL
¼ cup	light rum (optional)	50 mL

1. In a small saucepan, bring sugar and water to a boil, stirring to dissolve sugar. Reduce heat, and simmer for 5 minutes.
2. Add the lime zest. Remove from heat and let cool.
3. Stir in lime juice and rum (if desired).

Easy Breezy

FOR 4

Lemon Chicken

Rice Pilaf

Balsamic Tomato Platter

Banana-Almond Fool

Lemon Chicken

SERVES 4

Less lemon juice, more oil.

Oven: 400°F/200°C

Good

4	boneless, skinless chicken breasts	4
2	lemons *1/2 Lemon ?*	2
2	cloves garlic, crushed	2
1 tbsp.	olive oil	15 mL
1 tsp.	grated lemon zest	5 mL
1 tsp.	dried oregano	5 mL
1 tsp.	dried basil	5 mL
¼ tsp.	black pepper	1 mL
	Salt to taste	

1. Lightly spray with cooking spray a baking dish just large enough to hold the chicken. Place chicken in the dish.
2. Squeeze juice from lemons and pour into a jar. Add garlic, oil, lemon zest, oregano, basil, pepper and salt. Shake until well mixed.
3. Pour lemon mixture over chicken; marinate for 1 to 2 hours.
4. Bake, basting occasionally, for 45 minutes or until chicken is no longer pink inside.

Preparation Note

May also be cooked on the barbecue.

Rice Pilaf

SERVES 4

~~~~~~~~~~~~~~~~~~~~~~~~~~~~~~~~

Oven: 350°F/180°C

1½ tsp.	olive oil	7 mL
1	onion, finely chopped	1
1½ cups	long-grain rice	375 mL
2 cups	boiling chicken stock	500 mL
	Salt and pepper to taste	
½ cup	sliced mushrooms	125 mL
½ tsp.	olive oil	2 mL
	Chopped fresh parsley or coriander for garnish	

1. Heat 1 tsp. (5 mL) of the oil in a heavy pan over medium heat; sauté onion until golden.
2. Add rice, and stir until coated. Add boiling stock, salt and pepper.
3. Transfer mixture to a casserole dish. Cover and bake for 35 minutes or until liquid is absorbed and rice is cooked.
4. Sauté mushrooms in remaining ½ tsp./2 mL oil. Stir into rice mixture.
5. Garnish with parsley or coriander.

Preparation Note

This recipe can also be cooked on top of the stove. Bring rice to a full rolling boil; then reduce heat to low and simmer for 25 minutes or until rice is cooked. Stir in the sautéed mushrooms as above.

Vegetable stock may be substituted for chicken stock.

Balsamic Tomato Platter

2	medium tomatoes	2
1	cucumber	1
2 tbsp.	chopped fresh basil	30 mL
2 tbsp.	olive oil	30 mL
1 tbsp.	balsamic vinegar	15 mL

1. Slice tomatoes and cucumbers. Arrange on a platter.
2. Sprinkle with basil.
3. Mix oil and vinegar together; drizzle over the tomatoes and cucumbers.

Banana-Almond Fool

SERVES 4 TO 6

4	large bananas	4
	Zest and juice of 1 lemon	
	Zest and juice of 1 orange	
½ cup	toasted slivered almonds	125 mL
1 cup	no-fat plain yogurt	250 mL
⅓ cup	maple syrup	75 mL
2 tbsp.	brown sugar	30 mL

1. Mash the bananas by hand or in a food processor; add the lemon and orange juice.
2. Stir in half of the toasted almonds and half of the lemon and orange zest.
3. In a separate bowl, combine the yogurt and maple syrup. Stir into the banana mixture.
4. Pour mixture into individual serving dishes. Chill.
5. To serve, sprinkle ½ tsp. (2 mL) brown sugar on top of each bowl. Garnish with remaining almonds and zest.

Summer Salmon Sizzle

FOR 4

Romaine Mandarin Salad

Salmon on the Plank

Crunchy Brown Rice

Orange-Mango Asparagus

Strawberry Meringue

Romaine Mandarin Salad

1	small head romaine	1
1 can (10 oz.)	mandarin oranges, drained	1 can (284 mL)
1	small red onion, sliced in rings	1
⅓ cup	balsamic vinegar	75 mL
1 tbsp.	sugar	15 mL
1 tbsp.	olive oil	15 mL
	Salt and pepper to taste	

1. Tear lettuce into a bowl. Add oranges and onion.
2. In a jar combine vinegar, sugar, oil, salt and pepper; shake.
3. Pour dressing over salad and serve.

Salmon on the Plank

2	pieces cedar plank, each 6 inches x 10 inches x ¾ inch (15 cm x 25 cm x 2 cm)	2
4	fresh Atlantic salmon fillets, skinless	4
½ cup	olive oil	125 mL
	Lemon pepper	
	Salt	
	Lemon wedges	

1. Soak cedar planks in water for 30 minutes. While they are soaking, brush all sides of the salmon with olive oil; sprinkle very lightly with lemon pepper.
2. Pat dry cedar planks. Brush top (smooth side) and edges with remaining olive oil. Lightly sprinkle top of each plank with salt and lemon pepper.
3. Place 2 fillets on each cedar plank, on the seasoned smooth side.
4. Preheat barbecue to medium-low with lid closed.
5. Place planks on grill, at least 8 inches (20 cm) above coals. Cook at medium-low for 20 to 25 minutes or until fish is opaque. Do not turn fillets.
6. Remove fillets from cedar planks and serve immediately.

Note

Do not reuse cedar planks.

Crunchy Brown Rice

1 cup	brown rice	250 mL
½ cup	wild rice	125 mL
½ cup	raisins	125 mL
2 tsp.	canola oil	10 mL
1	onion, chopped	1
1	clove garlic, minced	1
2 tbsp.	minced fresh coriander	30 mL
½ cup	toasted chopped almonds	125 mL
	Salt and pepper to taste	

1. Cook brown rice according to package directions.
2. Cook wild rice according to package directions; drain if necessary.
3. Pour hot water over raisins, and let stand for a few minutes. Drain.
4. Heat oil in a large skillet over medium-high heat. Lightly stir-fry onion and garlic. Add brown rice and wild rice; fry several more minutes. Add the drained raisins.
5. Stir in the coriander, almonds, salt and pepper.
6. Serve immediately.

Orange-Mango Asparagus

SERVES 4 TO 6

1 tbsp.	olive oil	15 mL
2 tbsp.	grated fresh ginger	30 mL
1½ lb.	asparagus	750 g
¼ tsp.	salt	1 mL
½ cup	orange juice	125 mL
1	mango, peeled and sliced	1

1. Heat oil in large skillet over medium-high heat. Add ginger and sauté for 2 minutes.
2. Add asparagus, salt, orange juice and mango. Cover and cook until tender, about 5 minutes.

Strawberry Meringue

~~~~~~~~~~~~~~~~~~~~~~~~~~

Oven: 225°F/110°C

4	egg whites, at room temperature	4
¼ tsp.	cream of tartar	1 mL
	Pinch salt	
¾ cup	sugar	175 mL
	No-fat strawberry yogurt	
	Sliced fresh strawberries	
	and kiwi for garnish	

1. Beat egg whites, cream of tartar and salt until foamy.
2. Gradually beat in sugar and continue beating until egg whites are stiff and glossy.
3. Line a cookie sheet with parchment paper. Using a large spoon, drop 4 large mounds of meringue onto cookie sheet several inches apart. Flatten centre of each mound with rounded edge of spoon.
4. Bake for 1 hour. Turn off oven and let stand for 30 minutes in oven. Remove and let cool on a rack.
5. When meringues have cooled, carefully remove from cookie sheet and place each on a dessert plate. Top each meringue with a dollop of strawberry yogurt.
6. Garnish with slices of fresh strawberries and kiwi. Serve immediately.

The Elegant Lamb

FOR 6

Three-Vinegar Chunky Gazpacho

BBQ Butterflied Leg of Lamb

Tangy Potato Salad

Garlic and Tomato Pepper Kabobs

Grilled Portobello Mushrooms

Pavlova

Three-Vinegar Chunky Gazpacho

SERVES 6

6 cups	chopped tomatoes	1.5 L
2	medium cucumbers, coarsely chopped	2
1	green pepper, chopped	1
1¼ cups	chopped Vidalia onion	300 mL
1 cup	finely chopped celery	250 mL
1 can (48 oz.)	low-sodium tomato juice	1 can (1.36 L)
1 tbsp.	olive oil	15 mL
1 tbsp.	balsamic vinegar	15 mL
1 tbsp.	rice vinegar	15 mL
1 tbsp.	red wine vinegar	15 mL
1 tbsp.	dried basil (or ½ cup/125 mL chopped fresh)	15 mL
3	cloves garlic, minced	3

1. Combine all ingredients in a large bowl. Stir well.
2. Cover and chill.

Serving Suggestion

Serve with garlic croutons.

BBQ Butterflied Leg of Lamb

SERVES 6

1 tbsp.	grated orange zest	15 mL
½ cup	orange juice	125 mL
½ cup	dry white wine	125 mL
¼ cup	light soy sauce	50 mL
1 tbsp.	grated fresh ginger	15 mL
1 tsp.	dried thyme	5 mL
1 tsp.	black pepper	5 mL
1	butterflied leg of lamb (4–5 lb./2–2.5 kg)	1

1. Combine orange zest and juice, wine, soy sauce, ginger, thyme and pepper in a jar and shake well to mix.
2. Pour mixture over lamb in a large shallow glass or enamel pan. Cover and refrigerate overnight, turning lamb occasionally.
3. Drain lamb, reserving the marinade.
4. Barbecue on a lightly greased grill 4 to 5 inches (10 to 12 cm) from the coals, turning lamb occasionally and basting with the reserved marinade, for 1 hour or until well browned but still pink in the centre.
5. Slice thinly and serve immediately.

Note

For a butterflied leg, have the butcher remove the bone and spread out flat. Frozen butterflied legs are also available.

Tangy Potato Salad

~~~~~~~~~~~~~~~~~~~~~~~~~~~~~~~~~~~~~

1 cup	low-fat cottage cheese	250 mL
⅓ cup	skim milk	75 mL
¼ cup	white vinegar	50 mL
1 tbsp.	celery seed	15 mL
1 tsp.	dry mustard	5 mL
8 cups	cubed cooked potatoes, cooled	2 L
1 cup	sliced green onions	250 mL
1 cup	diced celery	250 mL
3 tbsp.	chopped fresh parsley	45 mL
	Salt and pepper to taste	

1. Combine cottage cheese, milk, vinegar, celery seed and mustard in a blender and process until smooth. (Or beat in a bowl.)
2. In a large bowl, combine potatoes, cottage cheese mixture, green onions, celery, parsley, salt and pepper. Toss well.
3. Cover and chill for at least 1 hour.

Garlic and Tomato Pepper Kabobs

~~~~~~~~~~~~~~~~~~~~~~

2	green peppers, cut in 1-inch (2.5 cm) squares	2
18	cloves garlic	18
18	cherry tomatoes	18
	Olive oil	

1. On a baking sheet, place green pepper squares and garlic cloves under broiler for 2 minutes or until golden but still firm. Cool.
2. Alternate cherry tomatoes, peppers and garlic cloves on skewers.
3. Brush kabobs with olive oil and grill approximately 4 inches (10 cm) above coals, several minutes on each side. Serve immediately.

Grilled Portobello Mushrooms

~~~~~~~~~~~~~~~~~~~~~~~~

2 tbsp.	soy sauce	30 mL
2 tbsp.	Worcestershire sauce	30 mL
2 tbsp.	liquid honey	30 mL
4	cloves garlic, crushed	4
6	large Portobello mushroom caps	6

1. Combine soy sauce, Worcestershire sauce, liquid honey and garlic.
2. Place mushroom caps on broiling pan and with a sharp knife score each cap in a crisscross pattern.
3. Baste mushrooms with sauce several times.
4. Place under grill or on barbecue for 2 to 3 minutes. Serve immediately.

Pavlova

~~~~~~~~~~~~~~~~~~~~~

Oven: 275°F/140°C

8	egg whites	8
1 cup	sugar	250 mL
1 tsp.	cornstarch	5 mL
1 tsp.	vanilla	5 mL
1 cup	no-fat yogurt	250 mL
¼ cup	maple syrup	50 mL
2 cups	sliced strawberries	500 mL
2	kiwis, peeled and sliced	2
2	bananas, sliced	2
½ cup	toasted slivered almonds	125 mL

1. Line a cookie sheet with parchment paper or foil. Draw a 10-inch (25 cm) circle (invert a plate on the paper and trace around it).
2. Beat egg whites until they start to form peaks.
3. Gradually beat in sugar, cornstarch and vanilla. Beat until stiff, glossy peaks form.
4. Spoon meringue onto the paper and spread evenly within the circle. Make the sides higher, with a dip in the centre.
5. Bake for 2 hours. Turn off heat and leave meringue in oven overnight. Next day, peel off paper or foil.
6. To serve, combine yogurt and maple syrup. Spread over the meringue.
7. Decorate with the sliced fruit. Chill until ready to serve.
8. Top with toasted almonds. Cut into wedges.

Family Get-Together

FOR 20

Sangria

Centrepiece Salad

Ginger-Orange Mould

(Sliced Tomatoes, Onions and Cucumbers)

"In the Pink" Potato Salad

Greek Pasta Salad

Corn Salad with Lime Dressing

Glorious Glazed Ham

(Whole-Wheat Rolls)

(Watermelon Wedges)

Raspberry-Chocolate Bombe

Slightly Skinny Fudgy Brownies

Sangria

SERVES 20

~~~~~~~~~~~~~~~~~~~~~

12	oranges	12
12	lemons	12
40	ice cubes	40
1½ cups	sugar	375 mL
6 bottles (26 oz.)	dry red wine	6 bottles (750 mL)
6 bottles (26 oz.)	soda water	6 bottles (750 mL)

1. Juice 6 oranges and 6 lemons; set juice aside. Thinly slice remaining oranges and lemons.
2. Place ice in a large punch bowl.
3. Add orange and lemon juice and slices and sugar. Stir.
4. When ready to serve, add wine and soda water; stir vigorously.
5. Taste and adjust sweetness.

Serving Suggestion

Be sure each glass gets ice and a piece of fruit.

Centrepiece Salad

1½ lb.	yellow beans, cut in 1-inch (2.5 cm) lengths	750 g
3 lb.	green beans, cut in 1-inch (2.5 cm) lengths	1.5 kg
3 lb.	carrots, sliced on the diagonal	1.5 kg
2 cans (14 oz.)	red kidney beans, rinsed and drained	2 cans (398 mL)
2	large red onions, sliced in rings	2
2	large green peppers, sliced in rings	2
	Worcestershire Dressing (page 100)	

1. Boil yellow beans, green beans and carrots separately until tender but still crunchy. Drain each vegetable and cool.
2. Arrange yellow beans, green beans, carrots and kidney beans in rows on a large oval platter.
3. Top with onion and green pepper rings.
4. Pour dressing over salad. Refrigerate for 3 to 4 hours.

Worcestershire Dressing

Yields 1½ cups/375 mL

½ cup	olive oil	125 mL
⅓ cup	white wine vinegar	75 mL
⅓ cup	apple juice	75 mL
1 tsp.	Worcestershire sauce	5 mL
¼ cup	sugar	50 mL
1	clove garlic, minced	1
½ tsp.	salt	2 mL
	Pinch pepper	

1. Combine all ingredients and blend well.

Ginger-Orange Mould

SERVES 20

2 packages (6 oz.)	lemon gelatine	2 packages (170 g)
2 tsp.	ginger	10 mL
1 tsp.	onion powder	5 mL
3 cups	boiling water	750 mL
1 can (10 oz.)	mandarin oranges	1 can (284 mL)
1 can (10 oz.)	water chestnuts, drained and thinly sliced	1 can (284 mL)
	Curly endive	
	Grapes	

1. Combine gelatine, ginger and onion powder in a large bowl. Stir in boiling water until gelatine dissolves.
2. Drain syrup from the mandarin oranges into a measuring cup; add enough cold water to equal 3 cups (750 mL) liquid. Stir into gelatine mixture.
3. Chill until as thick as unbeaten egg whites, about 1½ hours.
4. Fold in oranges and water chestnuts. Pour into an 8-cup (2 L) bundt pan or jelly mould. Chill until firm.
5. Turn out onto a large platter. Frame the base with curly endive. Fill the centre with some grapes.

Preparation Note

To make unmoulding easier, grease the pan or mould and place it in freezer while preparing the gelatine.

"In the Pink" Potato Salad

~~~~~~~~~~~~~~~~~~~~~~~~~~

5 lb.	potatoes	2.5 kg
3 cans (14 oz.)	sliced beets	3 cans (398 mL)
2 cups	no-fat sour cream	500 mL
¼ cup	cider vinegar	50 mL
	Salt and pepper to taste	
	Chopped fresh chives	

1. Cook potatoes; drain and slice. Place in a large bowl.
2. Drain beets, reserving ¼ cup (50 mL) of the juice. Add beets to potatoes.
3. Mix sour cream, vinegar, beet juice, salt and pepper. Pour over salad and toss.
4. Chill well. Serve garnished with chives.

Greek Pasta Salad

~~~~~~~~~~~~~~~~~~~~~~

5 cups	penne	1.25 L
1 cup	chopped celery	250 mL
1	green pepper, chopped	1
1	red pepper, chopped	1
1	onion, chopped	1
3	large tomatoes, chopped	3
1 cup	sliced black olives	250 mL
1 cup	crumbled light feta cheese	250 mL
	Salt and pepper to taste	
	Oil and Vinegar Dressing (page 104)	

1. Cook pasta in boiling salted water; drain. Cool pasta under cold water; drain. Transfer to a salad bowl.
2. Add chopped celery, peppers, onion, tomatoes, olives, feta cheese, salt, pepper and the Oil and Vinegar Dressing. Mix well.
3 Chill before serving.

Oil and Vinegar Dressing

Yields ⅔ cup/150 mL

½ cup	olive oil	125 mL
½ cup	white vinegar	125 mL
3	cloves garlic, minced	3
1 tsp.	dried basil	5 mL
	Salt and pepper to taste	

1. Put all ingredients in a jar and shake well. Refrigerate until ready to use.

Corn Salad with Lime Dressing

SERVES 20

~~~~~~~~~~~~~~~~~~~~~

1 tsp.	minced garlic	5 mL
4 cups	corn kernels	1 L
½ cup	dry white wine	125 mL
1½ cups	finely diced green pepper	375 mL
½ cup	finely diced red onion	125 mL
¼ cup	chopped fresh coriander	50 mL
2 tbsp.	chopped fresh parsley	30 mL
	Salt and pepper to taste	
	Lime Dressing (below)	

1. In a large skillet over medium heat, sauté garlic and corn in the wine for 5 minutes. Place in a salad bowl.
2. Add the rest of the ingredients and toss with Lime Dressing.
3. Chill before serving.

Lime Dressing

4 tbsp.	rice wine vinegar	60 mL
2 tbsp.	lime juice	30 mL

1. Shake vinegar and lime juice together in a jar.

Glorious Glazed Ham

Oven: 350°F/180°C

1	ham (10–15 lb./5–7 kg)	1
	Orange Glazing Sauce (below)	

1. Place ham cut side down on a rack in a roasting pan.
2. Brush Orange Glazing Sauce over ham.
3. Bake for 2 to 2½ hours, basting frequently with the pan juices, until meat thermometer reads 165°F (75°C).
4. Let ham stand before slicing. It can be sliced, wrapped and refrigerated until served.

Orange Glazing Sauce

1 cup	orange marmalade	250 mL
½ cup	ginger ale	125 mL
1 tbsp.	Dijon mustard	15 mL
1 tbsp.	dark rum	15 mL
1	clove garlic, minced	1
1 tsp.	ginger	5 mL
½ tsp.	ground cloves	2 mL

1. Mix all ingredients together in a small bowl.

Raspberry-Chocolate Bombe

4 cups	raspberry sorbet	1 L
6 cups	no-fat vanilla frozen dessert, softened	1.5 L
4 tbsp.	amaretto	60 mL
4 oz.	bittersweet chocolate, coarsely grated	125 g
	Raspberry Sauce (page 17)	
	Fresh mint sprigs for garnish	

1. Press sorbet into the bottom and up the sides of a chilled 5-cup (1.25 L) mould. Freeze until firm.
2. Mix softened vanilla dessert, amaretto and grated chocolate. Spoon into the mould, smoothing the top. Cover and freeze.
3. When ready to serve, dip mould into hot water for a few seconds. Invert onto a plate and serve with Raspberry Sauce.
4. Garnish with fresh mint and serve immediately.

Slightly Skinny Fudgy Brownies

MAKES 20 PIECES

~~~~~~~~~~~~~~~~~~~~

Oven: 325°F/160°C

½ cup	light butter	125 mL
½ cup	sweetened applesauce	125 mL
1⅓ cups	cocoa	325 mL
3 cups	sugar	750 mL
6	egg whites	6
2	eggs	2
2 cups	all-purpose flour	500 mL
1 tsp.	baking powder	5 mL

1. Melt butter in a saucepan over medium-low heat. Stir in applesauce.
2. Stir in cocoa; cook 1 more minute.
3. Stir in sugar; cook 1 more minute. The mixture will almost form a ball and be difficult to stir. Remove from heat.
4. In a bowl, beat egg whites; beat in whole eggs.
5. Gradually pour egg mixture into chocolate mixture, stirring with a whisk until well blended.
6. Combine flour and baking powder; add to the chocolate mixture. Stir well.
7. Pour batter into a 9- x 13-inch (3.5 L) baking pan coated with cooking spray.
8. Bake for 30 minutes or until firm. Cool.
9. Cut into 20 pieces.

3
Party Time

Hors d'Oeuvres, Canapés,

Drinks

*T*HERE IS NO WAY to stop the hands of time, but here in Georgian Bay territory one thing has never changed over the years for us—any excuse for a party! No matter if just a few friends drop in or a large theme event happens, home-made parties are always a big hit at any time of the year around here.

Want some ideas? We've had fun reviving some of the old favourites like charades (for the song category, try acting out "I've Got the Hungries for Your Loving and I'm Waiting in Your Welfare Line"). We've been known to replace Dinner Bridge with Dinner Fish on the odd occasion, and any one of our fish menus will be the highlight of the evening. Try a joke party, where each guest must tell a joke in front of the others, and then everyone votes on the funniest joke of the evening. And a big favourite for years has been the Slide Party, where each guest is given four or five "expressions" with a slide film a few weeks before the event. On party night each guest shows his or her slides and we vote for the slide that best portrays the saying. Or, in fact, the one that evokes the biggest laugh! This has provided for some hilarious memories on film!

Quite often, a celebration will take place after a simple outdoor excursion with friends and family. Walking and hiking have become preferable to skiing and jogging these days. We have hiked to the top of the hill overlooking the Martyrs' Shrine and Midland Bay, and we have walked along what's left of the old railway tracks near Copelands Creek in search of wild leeks and fiddleheads. We have boated out to Hope Island for an afternoon on the Bay, and we have played bocci ball in the backyard by the pool. We've even been ice fishing on Penetang Bay in the middle of January!

In our Party Time section, we offer some finger foods with seafood and vegetables instead of the typical cheese trays. We also include both alcoholic and nonalcoholic beverages for your enjoyment. And we are especially happy to present two of our old favourites in lower-fat form: Slender Escargot Pâté, and Lean and Mean Oysters in Cream. We've also been told that a party becomes a "happening" when our famous GBG Antipasto is served. Have fun!

Hors d'Oeuvres, Canapés

Slender Escargot Pâté

Lean and Mean Oysters in Cream

Hummus

Crispy Appetizer Won Ton Cups

Marinated Mushrooms

Shrimp Vegetable Dip

Southwest Chili Corn Bake

GBG Antipasto

Salsa Dip

Millennium Almond Dip

Cinnamon Nuts

Spiced Nuts

Slender Escargot Pâté

3 tbsp.	light margarine	45 mL
2	cloves garlic, crushed	2
1 tbsp.	dry white wine	15 mL
1 can (7 oz.)	escargots, drained	1 can (199 mL)
8 oz.	light cream cheese, softened	250 g
1 tbsp.	chopped fresh parsley	15 mL
½ tsp.	dried dillweed	2 mL
1	green onion, chopped	1
	Black pepper to taste	

1. In a medium saucepan over medium heat, melt margarine in garlic and wine. Add escargots; cover and simmer 5 minutes, stirring occasionally.
2. Cut cheese into 1-inch (2.5 cm) cubes. Put in food processor or blender with parsley, dill and green onion.
3. Add escargot mixture and black pepper; process 30 seconds.
4. Transfer pâté to serving dish. Chill.

Serving Suggestion

Serve with rice crackers or Melba toast.

Lean and Mean Oysters in Cream

YIELDS 1½ CUPS / 375 ML

~~~~~~~~~~~~~~~~~~~~~~

1 can (3 ⅔ oz.)	smoked oysters or mussels	1 can (104 g)
2 tsp.	lemon juice	10 mL
8 oz.	light cream cheese, softened	250 g
2 tbsp.	low-fat mayonnaise	30 mL
	Pinch pepper	
3	dashes hot pepper sauce	3

1. Drain oysters. Chop fine; sprinkle with lemon juice.
2. Cream the cheese. Beat in mayonnaise, pepper and hot pepper sauce until light and creamy.
3. Stir in chopped oysters. Taste and adjust seasoning.
4. Cover and refrigerate until ready to serve.

Serving Suggestion

Nice served on a mild-tasting cracker or Melba round.

Hummus

YIELDS 1 ½ CUPS / 375 ML

1 can (19 oz.)	chickpeas, rinsed and drained	1 can (540 mL)
¼ cup	tahini (sesame paste) or low-fat peanut butter	50 mL
1 tsp.	ground cumin	5 mL
4	cloves garlic, minced	4
2 tbsp.	lemon juice	30 mL
3 tbsp.	warm water	45 mL
	Freshly ground pepper to taste	

1. Combine all ingredients in food processor until well blended.
2. Serve hummus in a bowl in centre of platter surrounded with pita bread strips or pita chips.

Preparation Note

For a variation, add ¼ cup (50 mL) Mother's Spiced Tomato Sauce (page 168).

Crispy Appetizer Won Ton Cups

SERVES 6

Oven: 350°F/180°C

| 18 | won ton wrappers | 18 |

1. Cut won tons into circles with a 3-inch (8 cm) round cookie cutter.
2. Coat mini muffin pans with cooking spray.
3. Place 1 circle in each muffin cup; press to sides to mould won ton to cup.
4. Spray each won ton with cooking spray.
5. Bake for 6 to 8 minutes or until golden brown.
6. Fill with your favourite filling.

Preparation Note

Cups can be frozen in plastic bags until ready to use.

Serving Suggestion

Fill cups with light cream cheese and pepper jelly, hummus, lemon curd, curried crab or vanilla pudding topped with a strawberry.

Marinated Mushrooms

SERVES 8

~~~~~~~~~~~~~~~~~~~~~~~~~~~~~~

2 cans (10 oz.)	whole button mushrooms	2 cans (284 mL)
	Sodium-reduced light	
	soy sauce	

1. Drain mushrooms, reserving liquid from 1 can.
2. Place mushrooms and reserved liquid in large jar.
3. Add enough soy sauce to cover mushrooms.
4. Cover jar and shake gently to combine liquids.
5. Refrigerate overnight. Drain before serving. Serve at room temperature.

Preparation Note

A garlic clove can be added.

Shrimp Vegetable Dip

YIELDS 1 ½ CUPS / 375 ML

~~~~~~~~~~~~~~~~~~~~~~~~~~~~~~

4 oz.	light cream cheese	125 g
3–4 tbsp.	no-fat mayonnaise	45–60 mL
1 can (6.5 oz.)	small shrimp, drained	1 can (184 g)
2	green onions, chopped	2
	Salt and pepper to taste	
	Paprika	

1. Whip together cream cheese and mayonnaise.
2. Stir in shrimp, green onions, salt and pepper.
3. Place in serving dish and sprinkle with paprika.

Preparation Note

You may substitute crab meat.

Serving Suggestion

Serve with a tray of mixed raw vegetables.

119

Southwest Chili Corn Bake

Oven: 300°F/150°C

1 can (14 oz.)	corn kernels	1 can (398 mL)
1 can (14 oz.)	creamed corn	1 can (398 mL)
8 oz.	light cream cheese	250 g
1 can (4 oz.)	chopped green chilies	1 can (125 g)
1 cup	cornflake crumbs	250 mL

1. Spray a 7- x 11-inch (2 L) casserole dish with cooking spray.
2. Combine corn kernels and creamed corn in a saucepan.
3. Cut cream cheese into cubes and stir into corn. Heat over low heat, stirring, until cheese melts.
4. Add chilies and stir well. Pour mixture into casserole dish. Top with cornflakes.
5. Bake for 15 minutes or until lightly browned.

Serving Suggestion

Serve with nacho chips or pita crisps.

GBG Antipasto

4	large carrots, chopped	4
2	large green peppers, chopped	2
1	large red pepper, chopped	1
1	jalapeno pepper, chopped (optional)	1
2 cans (14 oz.)	pitted black olives, chopped	2 cans (398 mL)
1 jar (14 oz.)	broken green olives	1 jar (398 mL)
2 cans (14 oz.)	artichokes, chopped	2 cans (398 mL)
2 jars (14 oz.)	pickled onions, chopped	2 jars (398 mL)
1 jar (48 oz.)	sweet mixed pickles, chopped	1 jar (1.36 L)
1 tbsp.	olive oil	15 mL
1	large cauliflower, cut into bite-sized pieces	1
5	cloves garlic, crushed	5
1 bottle (4 cups)	ketchup	1 bottle (1 L)
1 cup	dry red wine	250 mL
½ cup	water	125 mL
1 can (10 oz.)	tomato paste	1 can (284 mL)
1 tbsp.	dried oregano	15 mL
2 cans (10 oz.)	mushroom pieces	2 cans (284 mL)
3 cans (6.5 oz.)	flaked tuna in water (optional)	3 cans (184 g)

1. In a large, heavy pot, combine the carrots, green and red peppers, jalapeno (if desired), black and green olives, artichokes, pickled onions and sweet pickles.

(continued)

2. Heat olive oil in a frying pan. Add the cauliflower and garlic. Sauté 3 to 4 minutes. Remove from heat and add to the vegetable mixture.
3. In a bowl, combine the ketchup, wine, water, tomato paste and oregano. Pour into the vegetable mixture. Bring to a boil, stirring frequently.
4. Add the mushrooms and tuna (if desired). Stir until well combined. Cover and simmer for 20 minutes, stirring frequently to prevent sticking. If it appears to be too thick, add a little more water.
5. Place mixture in hot sterilized jars. Seal jars. Keep in refrigerator or freeze.

Preparation Note

This is one of our favourite gifts to make around the Christmas season for friends. The recipe can be cut in half to make a smaller quantity.

Serving Suggestion

Serve on crackers of your choice.

Salsa Dip

YIELDS 2 CUPS / 500 ML

4	tomatoes	4
½ cup	chopped green pepper	125 mL
¼ cup	minced onion	50 mL
1–2 tsp.	dried coriander	5–10 mL
2 tsp.	lime or lemon juice	10 mL
2	cloves garlic, minced	2
1	small hot chili, minced	1
	Salt and pepper to taste	

1. Coarsely chop tomatoes. Put in a food processor with green pepper and onion. Process briefly to combine vegetables but do not purée.
2. Add remaining ingredients and blend once more. If watery, strain slightly.
3. Serve with nacho chips.

Millennium Almond Dip

SERVES 6

~~~~~~~~~~~~~~~~~~~~~~~~~~~~~~

4 oz.	light cream cheese	125 g
1 cup	no-fat sour cream	250 mL
¼ tsp.	almond extract	1 mL
½ tsp.	vanilla	2 mL
3 tbsp.	maple syrup	45 mL

1. Combine all ingredients in a food processor or blender. Blend until smooth. Pour into a serving dish.

Serving Suggestion

Cube your favourite fruit and arrange on a large platter. Place dip in the centre. Dip fruit with toothpicks or fondue forks.

Cinnamon Nuts

YIELDS 5 CUPS / 1.25 L

~~~~~~~~~~~~~~~~~~~~~~~~~~~~~~

Oven: 325°F/160°C

2	egg whites	2
4 cups	salted peanuts	1 L
⅓ cup	sugar	75 mL
4 tsp.	cinnamon	20 mL
1 tsp.	nutmeg	5 mL
	Pinch salt	
1 cup	raisins	250 mL

1. In a large bowl, beat egg whites until slightly frothy. Add nuts and coat well with egg white.
2. Combine sugar, cinnamon, nutmeg and salt. Pour over nuts. Stir well.
3. Lightly spray a baking sheet with cooking spray. Spread nuts evenly on baking sheet. Bake for 15 minutes, stirring occasionally to prevent burning. Do not overcook.
4. Remove from oven and stir in raisins. Cool.

Spiced Nuts

YIELDS 3 CUPS / 750 ML

Oven: 350°F/180°C

2 tbsp.	water	30 mL
1 tbsp.	olive oil	15 mL
4 tbsp.	brown sugar	60 mL
1	clove garlic, minced	1
1 tsp.	salt	5 mL
½ tsp.	ground cumin	2 mL
1 tsp.	ground coriander	5 mL
4 tsp.	chili powder	20 mL
3 cups	mixed salted nuts	750 mL

1. Heat water, oil and brown sugar in a large frying pan over medium-high heat.
2. Add garlic; stir-fry for 1 minute or until mixture is bubbly.
3. Turn off heat. Stir in rest of seasonings. Mix well.
4. Add the nuts. Stir until coated. Lightly spray a baking sheet with cooking spray. Spread nuts on baking sheet. Bake 15 minutes, stirring occasionally to prevent burning. Do not overcook.
5. Remove from oven and cool.

Preparation Note

Use the milder Mexican chili powder, not the hot Asian kind.

Drinks

Lemonade Syrup

Slush

Frozen Watermelon Daiquiris

Grapefruit Mist

Fruity Tofu Smoothy

Ron's Party Pail

Pink Lemonade Slush

Peter's Caesar

Tropical Night

Lemonade Syrup

YIELDS 2 CUPS / 500 ML

~~~~~~~~~~~~~~~~~~~~~~~

2 cups	sugar	500 mL
1 cup	water	250 mL
	Rind of 2 lemons, cut in thin strips	
	Juice of 6 lemons	

1. Boil sugar, water and lemon rind for 5 minutes. Strain and discard rind. Cool.
2. Add lemon juice. Store in refrigerator.
3. To serve, use 2 tbsp. (30 mL) of lemon syrup for each 1 cup (250 mL) of water.

Slush

YIELDS 5 CUPS / 1.25 L

~~~~~~~~~~~~~~~~~~~~~~~~

2 cups	coarsely chopped cantaloupe	500 mL
2	bananas, sliced	2
2 cups	pineapple-orange juice	500 mL
1 tbsp.	sugar	15 mL
1 tbsp.	lime juice	15 mL

1. Freeze cantaloupe and banana.
2. Place frozen fruit in food processor. Process until chunky.
3. With processor on, slowly add remaining ingredients, and process until smooth.

Frozen Watermelon Daiquiris

SERVES 12

~~~~~~~~~~~~~~~~~~~~~~~~~~~~~

10 cups	cubed seeded watermelon	2.5 L
1 cup	sugar	250 mL
1 cup	lime juice	250 mL
¾ cup	white rum (optional)	175 mL
	Mint leaves for garnish	

1. In a food processor and working in batches, process watermelon, sugar, lime juice and rum (if desired) until slushy. Pour into a large bowl.
2. Freeze at least 3 hours or overnight until thick and slushy.
3. Spoon into glasses and garnish with mint leaves.

Preparation Note

If mixture is frozen overnight, you may have to let it stand at room temperature for 20 minutes or so to thaw slightly.

Grapefruit Mist

YIELDS 7 CUPS / 1.75 L

1 bottle (26 oz.)	ginger ale	1 bottle (750 mL)
1 can (19 oz.)	grapefruit juice	1 can (540 mL)
1½ cups	apple juice	375 mL
¼ cup	lemon juice	50 mL
2 tbsp.	sugar	30 mL

1. Mix all ingredients together.
2. Serve with ice.

Fruity Tofu Smoothy

1 package (19 oz.)	silken tofu	1 package (539 g)
1 can (8 oz.)	crushed pineapple	1 can (227 mL)
10	whole fresh or frozen strawberries	10
2	bananas	2
½–1 cup	orange juice	125–250 mL

1. Blend tofu, pineapple and strawberries in blender or food processor until smooth.
2. Add bananas and blend.
3. Blend in enough orange juice until mixture is smooth and the desired consistency.

Preparation Note

Try any fresh fruit in season. Will keep in the refrigerator.

Ron's Party Pail

SERVES 20

~~~~~~~~~~~~~~~~~~~~~~~~~~~~~~~~

1 bottle (8 cups)	7-Up	1 bottle (2 L)
1 bottle (4 cups)	cranberry juice	1 bottle (1 L)
1 can (12. oz.)	frozen orange juice concentrate	1 can (341 mL)
3 cups	white rum	750 mL
½ cup	peach schnapps	125 mL
	Mint leaves and orange slices for garnish	

1. Mix all ingredients in a pail and freeze.
2. To serve, ladle into glasses. Decorate each glass with mint and an orange slice.

Pink Lemonade Slush

SERVES 2

1 can (12 oz.)	frozen pink lemonade	1 can (355 mL)
1½ cups	ice cubes	375 mL
⅓ cup	vodka or gin	75 mL

1. Place all ingredients in a blender and blend until slushy.

Preparation Note

More ice or liquor can be added to suit your taste.

Peter's Caesar

~~~~~~

½	lemon, cut in 2 wedges	½
1 tbsp.	seasoning salt	15 mL
1 tbsp.	celery salt	15 mL
4	ice cubes	4
1–2 oz.	vodka	30–55 mL
	Garlic Tabasco sauce	
	Tabasco sauce	
	Worcestershire sauce	
	Clamato juice	

1. Moisten rim of glass with one lemon wedge.
2. Combine seasoning salt and celery salt on a plate and dip glass into mixture to coat moistened rim.
3. Squeeze juice of remaining lemon wedge into glass. Add 4 ice cubes and vodka.
4. Add 3 or 4 dashes garlic Tabasco and 1 dash regular Tabasco.
5. Add 3 or 4 dashes Worcestershire sauce, or to taste.
6. Fill glass with Clamato juice. Stir and enjoy.

Serving Suggestion

A celery stalk may be added to the drink before serving, although Peter prefers to "hold the salad."

Tropical Night

~~~~~~

⅔ cup	frozen peach punch concentrate	150 mL
⅔ cup	frozen orange juice concentrate	150 mL
½ package	orange/pineapple Kool-Aid	½ package
⅓ cup	sugar	75 mL
⅓ cup	water	75 mL
18	ice cubes	18
	Banana slices for garnish	

1. In a blender, mix all ingredients until smooth. If you want a crunchy drink, do not blend as long.
2. Pour into cups and garnish with banana slices.

Serving Suggestion

For a great taste, take a fresh pineapple and cut the fruit out of the middle. Pour the Tropical Night into the pineapple and serve with straws.

Three members of the Students Against Drunk Drivers at Midland Secondary School entered a county-wide competition to create a nonalcoholic beverage. Congratulations to Danielle Tindale, Melissa Coleman and Angela Brewer ("The Mix-Aholics") for their First Prize drink, Tropical Night.

4

Mix and Match

Soups

In-Betweens

Salads

Pickles

*A*LTHOUGH IT IS USUALLY OUR STYLE to offer you tasty and nutritious recipes in menu format, we have also chosen to devote one section of this book to the pickers and choosers of the culinary world! Here we offer a selection of soups, salads and one-pot meals that can be mixed and matched depending on the occasion and the time available for cooking. We also provide a very special array of pickles and preserves to choose from when you are designing your own menu.

This section will appeal to vegetarians and non-vegetarians, to big eaters and small eaters, to the seasoned cook and the inexperienced cook, and to young people and the rest of us! If you have the makings for one of our soups or one-pot meals, then you can ask "Would you like to stay for dinner?" with pleasure, not panic! Or, if it's your turn to feed a hungry group, any of these "meal-in-one" selections can simmer while you are out enjoying a Georgian Bay day, and please the hearty appetite when you return.

With the help of this chapter, we invite you to be brave ... be bold ... take a salad from here and match it with a soup from somewhere else in our book. Pick a one-pot dish from this selection and serve it with a bread recipe from another menu. Choose our Risotto with Mushrooms, Onions and Brandy and you won't need anything else but a good bottle of wine!

A word about pickling and preserving. Years ago, our mothers and grandmothers needed to preserve fresh foods because the growing season was so short. Today we preserve because we like to share the fruits of our labour with our families and friends: a pot of jelly for a special someone here, a jar of chutney to take to a host there. And we offer our gifts with pride, since the ingredients usually come from our own gardens. Our Perkinsfield Tomato Relish is a wonderful accompaniment to any meat dish, and you must try Annie P's Watermelon Rind Pickles with just about anything. We've offered Mrs. B's Dilled Green Tomatoes as a light and tasty before-dinner treat, and Jessie's Pickled Beets are a traditional summertime favourite. (Yes, our Prize-Winning Bread and Butter Pickles really did win first prize two years in a row at the Midland Fall Fair.) No matter what the recipe, or where it originated, when the makings come from the soil near Georgian Bay, and the labour is filled with love, then the gift will be truly appreciated in anyone's home.

"Food has become a utensil for all our favourite condiments."

Soups

Curried Corn and Red Pepper Chowder

Barley Lentil Soup

Quick Oriental Ground Pork Soup

D's Mushroom Soup

Souper Toot Soup

Chicken Corn Chowder

Barb's Healing Soup

Curried Corn and Red Pepper Chowder

SERVES 8

1 tbsp.	butter	15 mL
1 cup	chopped onion	250 mL
2	cloves garlic, minced	2
1 tbsp.	all-purpose flour	15 mL
2 cups	chicken stock	500 mL
2 cups	water	500 mL
2	potatoes, diced	2
2 cups	corn kernels	500 mL
1 cup	chopped red pepper	250 mL
½ cup	skim milk powder	125 mL
2 tsp.	curry powder	10 mL
1 tsp.	ground cumin	5 mL
1 tbsp.	chopped fresh coriander	15 mL

1. Melt butter in a soup pot. Add onions and garlic; sauté until onions are translucent.
2. Sprinkle flour into pot and stir well.
3. Slowly stir in chicken stock and water.
4. Add potatoes; simmer until they are tender.
5. Add corn and red peppers; simmer for 10 minutes.
6. Add skim milk powder, curry powder and cumin, stirring quickly. Heat through.
7. To serve, ladle into bowls; garnish each bowl with coriander.

Barley Lentil Soup

~~~~~~

2 cups	lentils	500 mL
9 cups	water	2.25 L
2 cups	vegetable broth	500 mL
½ cup	pearl barley	125 mL
1½ cups	chopped onion	375 mL
1 cup	chopped celery	250 mL
1	green pepper, chopped	1
3	cloves garlic, crushed	3
2	bay leaves	2
	Dash cayenne pepper	
½ tsp.	dried thyme	2 mL
½ tsp.	ground cumin (or to taste)	2 mL
2 tbsp.	balsamic vinegar	30 mL
1 can (28 oz.)	chopped tomatoes	1 can (796 mL)
	Salt and pepper to taste	

1. Simmer lentils, 6 cups (1.5 L) water and vegetable broth for about 2 hours.
2. In a separate pot, simmer barley and 3 cups (750 mL) water for 30 minutes or until cooked.
3. Add the barley and the rest of the ingredients to the lentil mixture; simmer 1 more hour. Discard bay leaves before serving.

Quick Oriental Ground Pork Soup

SERVES 6 TO 8

1 lb.	ground pork	500 g
1	egg, lightly beaten	1
1	green onion, minced	1
1	clove garlic, minced	1
1 tbsp.	soy sauce	15 mL
2 tsp.	grated fresh ginger	10 mL
1 tsp.	sesame oil	5 mL
1 tsp.	pepper	5 mL
8 cups	chicken stock	2 L
3	slices fresh ginger	3
1	clove garlic, crushed	1
1 package (16 oz.)	frozen Oriental vegetables	1 package (500 g)
	Sliced green onions for garnish	

1. In a medium bowl, combine pork, egg, green onion, minced garlic, soy sauce, grated ginger, sesame oil and pepper. Blend well. Set mixture aside.
2. In a large soup pot, bring chicken stock, sliced ginger and crushed garlic to a boil. Reduce heat to low; simmer 15 minutes.
3. Add frozen vegetables. Return to a boil.
4. Drop heaping teaspoons of pork mixture into soup; simmer until meatballs cook through, 10 to 15 minutes.
5. To serve, garnish with sliced green onions.

D's Mushroom Soup

~~~~~~

3 tbsp.	applesauce	45 mL
5 tbsp.	all-purpose flour	75 mL
2 tbsp.	olive oil	30 mL
3 cups	vegetable broth	750 mL
½ tsp.	dried thyme	2 mL
2 tbsp.	vegetable broth	30 mL
1½ lb.	mushrooms, sliced	750 g
2 tbsp.	chopped fresh parsley	30 mL
	Salt and pepper to taste	
1½ cups	skim milk	350 mL

1. In a large saucepan over medium heat, whisk together applesauce, 3 tbsp. (45 mL) of the flour and 1 tbsp. (15 mL) of the oil.
2. Whisk in broth slowly to thicken. Add thyme; cook for 3 minutes, stirring constantly. Set aside.
3. Combine remaining 1 tbsp. (15 mL) oil and the vegetable broth in a frying pan over medium heat. Add mushrooms; sauté for 15 minutes or until soft. Add parsley, salt and pepper. Add to first mixture.
4. Mix remaining 2 tbsp. (30 mL) flour and ¼ cup (50 mL) milk in a jar. Shake until smooth. Stir into soup.
5. Add the last 1¼ cups (300 mL) of milk. Continue to cook over low heat until slightly thickened and hot.

Preparation Note

You can also use skim milk powder in cream soups. Just add the powder to stock or soup liquid. Blend in blender or food processor.

Souper Toot Soup

SERVES 8

~~~~~~~~~~~~~~~~~~~~~~

2 cups	mixed dried beans	500 mL
½ cup	pearl barley	125 mL
2 cups	vegetable broth	500 mL
1½ tsp.	celery seed	7 mL
1 tsp.	chili powder	5 mL
½ tsp.	garlic powder	2 mL
½ tsp.	dried chives	5 mL
½ tsp.	dried tarragon	5 mL
½ tsp.	salt	2 mL
¼ tsp.	allspice	1 mL
¼ tsp.	pepper	1 mL
1 cup	chopped onion	250 mL
1 cup	chopped celery	250 mL
1 cup	diced potato	250 mL

1. Cover beans in water and soak overnight. Drain.
2. Cook barley in water according to package instructions until water is absorbed. Set aside.
3. Simmer the beans in vegetable broth and 6 cups (1.5 L) water for 1 hour or until beans are cooked. Add more water or vegetable broth as necessary.
4. Add seasonings, vegetables and barley. Simmer for 30 minutes. Taste and adjust seasonings.

Chicken Corn Chowder

~~~~~~

1 tbsp.	butter	15 mL
1 cup	sliced mushrooms	250 mL
¼ cup	all-purpose flour	50 mL
3½ cups	skim milk	875 mL
1 cup	chopped potatoes	250 mL
1 tsp.	dried thyme	5 mL
	Salt and pepper	
2 cups	frozen corn, thawed	500 mL
1½–2 cups	diced cooked chicken	375–500 mL
4	green onions, chopped	4
	Sliced green onion for garnish	

1. Melt butter in large saucepan over medium heat.
2. Add mushrooms and sauté 3 to 4 minutes.
3. Blend in flour with a whisk.
4. Gradually add milk, stirring constantly with the whisk.
5. Add potatoes, thyme, salt, pepper and corn. Bring to a boil.
6. Stir in chicken and chopped green onions. Cover and reduce heat. Simmer for 15 minutes.
7. Ladle soup into bowls. Garnish with sliced green onions.

Barb's Healing Soup

SERVES 8

Oven: 350°F/180°C

1	whole garlic bulb	1
1 tsp.	olive oil	5 mL
1	large sweet potato, cubed	1
2	potatoes, cubed	2
1	large carrot, sliced	1
1	large green pepper, chopped	1
1	large onion, chopped	1
10–12 cups	water	2.5–3 L
2	vegetable bouillon cubes	2
2 tsp.	dried basil	10 mL
	Salt and pepper to taste	

1. Wrap whole garlic bulb in foil with a few drops of water. Bake for 40 minutes.
2. Heat oil in a frying pan or saucepan; sauté vegetables for 3 to 5 minutes. Remove from heat.
3. Boil water in a large pot. Whisk in bouillon cubes. Squeeze garlic pulp into the water.
4. Add vegetables; bring to a boil. Reduce heat and simmer for 30 minutes or until vegetables are tender.
5. Stir in basil, salt and pepper and serve.

In-Betweens

Tomato Stir-Fry

Gussied-Up Spaghetti Sauce

*Risotto with Mushrooms,
Onions and Brandy*

Peppy Focaccia Sandwich

I Can't Believe It's Eggplant

Vegetarian Pizza

Bean Chili

Refried Beans

Diana's Rice and Vegetable Medley

Herb Quick Bread

Tomato Stir-Fry

~~~~~~~~~~~~~~~~~~~~~~~~~~

1 tsp.	olive oil	5 mL
2	onions, quartered	2
1	clove garlic, minced	1
6	tomatoes, diced	6
2 cups	sliced mushrooms	500 mL
1 tsp.	dried basil	5 mL
¼ tsp.	salt	1 mL
¼ tsp.	pepper (or to taste)	1 mL
½ cup	dry white wine	125 mL

1. In a large frying pan over medium-high heat, heat oil. Sauté onions and garlic 3 or 4 minutes.
2. Add tomatoes and mushrooms. Stir-fry 3 or 4 minutes more.
3. Add seasonings and wine. Continue to cook until slightly thickened.
4. Serve over hot penne or other pasta.

Gussied-Up Spaghetti Sauce

1 tbsp.	olive oil	15 mL
2 cups	sliced mushrooms	500 mL
½ cup	chopped onion	125 mL
1	clove garlic, minced	1
1 jar (28 oz.)	spaghetti sauce	1 jar (796 mL)
4	Soya Veggie Slices, chopped	4

1. Heat oil in a nonstick frying pan; sauté mushrooms and onions.
2. Add garlic; cook another minute.
3. Stir in spaghetti sauce and chopped Veggie Slices. Continue to cook until heated through.

Serving Suggestion

Serve over buckwheat pasta.

Risotto with Mushrooms, Onions and Brandy

SERVES 4 TO 6

3 tbsp.	olive oil	45 mL
1	large onion, diced	1
1	clove garlic, minced	1
¾ lb.	mushrooms (oyster, chanterelle), chopped	375 g
	Salt and pepper to taste	
¼ cup	brandy	50 mL
8 oz.	arborio rice (Italian rice)	250 g
1	bay leaf	1
3 cups	hot chicken or vegetable broth	750 mL
½ cup	light Parmesan cheese	125 mL

1. In a large, heavy skillet over medium-high heat, heat olive oil; sauté onion and garlic until golden.
2. Add mushrooms, salt and pepper; sauté until mushrooms are soft.
3. Turn up heat. Stir in brandy.
4. Add rice; sauté until light brown, approximately 5 minutes. Rice will be opaque.
5. Add bay leaf. Reduce heat to medium.

6. Add ½ cup (125 mL) chicken broth, stirring often so rice does not stick. Continue to stir until broth is absorbed, then add another ½ cup (125 mL) broth. Continue until rice is done. This usually takes from 15 to 20 minutes. Discard bay leaf.
7. Add Parmesan cheese, toss and serve.

Preparation Note

Risotto is Italy's comfort food. It has to be simmered slowly and constantly stirred so that it gradually absorbs all its flavourful cooking liquids.

Peppy Focaccia Sandwich

SERVES 6

~~~~~~~~~~~~~~~~~~~~~~~~~~~

Oven: 350°F/180°C

1	8-inch (20 cm) round focaccia	1
⅓ cup	light garden-vegetable cream cheese	75 mL
1	tomato, thinly sliced	1
½	green pepper, thinly sliced	½
	Fat-free Veggie Pepperoni	
1	small red onion, thinly sliced	1
¾ cup	shredded low-fat cheese	175 mL

1. Slice focaccia in half horizontally.
2. Spread each cut side with cream cheese.
3. Layer bottom half with tomato, pepper, pepperoni, onion and cheese. Cover with top half of the bread.
4. Wrap tightly in foil. Bake 15 to 20 minutes or until hot.
5. Cut into wedges.

I Can't Believe It's Eggplant!

Oven: 350°F/180°C

2	eggplants	2
2 tbsp.	olive oil	30 mL
2	green peppers, thinly sliced	2
1	large Spanish onion, thinly sliced	1
¼ cup	vegetable broth	50 mL
1 lb.	sliced mushrooms	500 g
3	large tomatoes, peeled, seeded and diced	3
3	cloves garlic, minced	3
2 tbsp.	chopped fresh parsley	30 mL
1 tbsp.	dried basil	15 mL
1 tsp.	dried oregano	5 mL
	Salt and pepper to taste	
1½ cups	bottled or canned spaghetti sauce	375 mL

1. Remove ends of eggplant and cut into ½-inch (1 cm) slices.
2. Heat 1 tbsp. (15 mL) of the oil in a large nonstick pan over medium-high heat. Brown eggplant in batches. Then arrange in a single layer in a 9- x 13-inch (3/3.5 L) baking dish sprayed with cooking spray.
3. Sauté peppers and onion in the rest of the oil and the vegetable broth.
4. Add mushrooms and continue to cook for approximately 3 minutes.
5. Add tomatoes, garlic, seasonings and spaghetti sauce. Cook another 10 minutes.
6. Spoon sauce over eggplant. Bake for 20 minutes and serve.

Vegetarian Pizza

~~~~~~~~~~~~~~~~~~~~~~~~~~~

Oven: 350°F/180°C

1 cup	meatless bottled spaghetti sauce	250 mL
1	large pizza crust	1
	Veggie Pepperoni	
1	green pepper, chopped	1
2 cups	sliced mushrooms	500 mL
1 cup	chopped onion	250 mL
	Crumbled feta cheese	

1. Spread sauce on pizza crust; place on baking sheet.
2. Cut pepperoni slices and place on pizza.
3. Sauté green pepper, mushrooms and onion in a large nonstick frying pan until soft.
4. Spread vegetables over pizza and top with feta.
5. Bake for 10 minutes or until cheese is golden.

Preparation Note

You may substitute Mozzarella-flavour Veggie Slices (a soya product) for feta cheese. Try whole-wheat pitas instead of pizza crust.

Bean Chili

1 cup	TVP (optional)	250 mL
2 cups	dried black-eyed peas	500 mL
6 cups	water	1.5 L
1 tbsp.	olive oil	15 mL
1	large onion, chopped	1
1	green pepper, chopped	1
3	cloves garlic, minced	3
2 cans (19 oz.)	chopped tomatoes	2 cans (540 mL)
2 tbsp.	chili powder (or to taste)	30 mL
	Salt and pepper to taste	

1. Soak TVP (if using) according to package directions.
2. Simmer beans in water for 30 minutes.
3. In a large frying pan over medium-high heat, heat oil. Sauté onion, green pepper and garlic for 3 minutes. Add to beans.
4. Stir in tomatoes, seasonings and TVP.
5. Simmer for 20 minutes. Add more water if necessary.

Preparation Note

TVP is textured vegetable protein—a soya meat substitute.

Refried Beans

SERVES 12

~~~~~~~~~~~~~~~~

4 cups	dried pinto beans	1 L
2 tbsp.	olive oil	30 mL
3 cups	chopped onion	750 mL
2 tbsp.	minced garlic	30 mL
1 cup	chopped green pepper	250 mL
½ tsp.	ground coriander	2 mL
4 tsp.	ground cumin	20 mL
½ tsp.	black pepper	2 mL
½ tsp.	salt	2 mL
	Spicy Sour Cream Sauce (below)	

1. Cover beans with water and soak overnight.
2. Drain beans. Simmer them in fresh water to cover for 1½ hours or until soft. Drain and mash.
3. Heat oil in a frying pan and sauté onion, garlic and green pepper until tender.
4. Stir in seasonings.
5. Add vegetable mixture to the mashed beans. Mix well.
6. Serve hot with a dollop of Spicy Sour Cream Sauce.

Spicy Sour Cream Sauce

Yields 2½ cups/625 mL

2 cups	no-fat sour cream	500 mL
½ cup	spicy salsa	125 mL

1. Mix sour cream and salsa together.

158

Diana's Rice and Vegetable Medley

SERVES 6

1 cup	brown rice	250 mL
½ cup	lentils	125 mL
½ cup	split peas	125 mL
5 cups	water	1.25 L
½ tsp.	salt (or salt substitute)	2 mL
½ tsp.	pepper	2 mL
1 cup	cooked diced carrots	250 mL
1 cup	cooked peas or green beans	250 mL
1 cup	corn kernels	250 mL
2 cups	chopped spinach	500 mL

1. In a large saucepan, combine rice, lentils, split peas and water. Bring to a boil. Cover and simmer for 30 minutes or until cooked and all water is absorbed.
2. Add salt and pepper.
3. Add vegetables to rice mixture; stir over medium heat until hot. Serve immediately.

Serving Suggestion

You can serve this dish as is, or you can use as a stuffing for green peppers or tomatoes baked at 350°F (180°C) in covered dish for 20 minutes.

Herb Quick Bread

Oven: 350°F/180°C

2½ cups	all-purpose flour	625 mL
1½ tsp.	baking soda	7 mL
1 tsp.	baking powder	5 mL
½ tsp.	salt	2 mL
½ tsp.	dried tarragon	2 mL
½ tsp.	dried basil	2 mL
½ tsp.	dried thyme	2 mL
½ tsp.	dried sage	2 mL
½ tsp.	onion powder	2 mL
1½ cups	buttermilk	375 mL
½ cup	apricot purée	125 mL

1. Lightly spray a 9- x 5-inch (2 L) loaf pan with cooking spray.
2. Sift together flour, baking soda, baking powder and salt. Add herbs and onion powder.
3. Combine buttermilk and apricot purée in a large bowl. Add the dry ingredients and mix well.
4. Spoon batter into loaf pan. Bake for 1 hour or until knife inserted in the centre of the loaf comes out clean.
5. Cool in pan for 10 minutes. Turn leaf out onto a rack to cool.

Preparation Note

You can use a small jar of baby food apricot purée.

Salads

Tomato and Bean Salad

Artichoke Black Bean Salad

Another Bean Salad

Ensalata Misto

*Mixed Green Salad
with Curry Dressing*

Tomato and Bean Salad

SERVES 8

~~~~~~~~~~~~~~~~~~~~~~~~~~~

1 can (14 oz.)	chickpeas	1 can (398 mL)
1 can (14 oz.)	black beans	1 can (398 mL)
4	medium tomatoes, seeded and chopped	4
¼ cup	chopped fresh basil	50 mL
¼ cup	fresh oregano (or 1 tsp./5 mL dried)	50 mL
3	green onions, chopped	3
3	cloves garlic, minced	3
½ tsp.	salt	2 mL
¼ tsp.	pepper	1 mL

1. Drain and rinse chickpeas and beans.
2. Combine all ingredients and let stand for several hours.
3. Serve on a bed of fresh greens.

Artichoke Black Bean Salad

~~~~~~

1 can (14 oz.)	black beans, rinsed and drained	1 can (398 mL)
⅔ cup	chopped red pepper	150 mL
¼ cup	chopped sweet onion	50 mL
1 jar (6 oz.)	marinated artichoke hearts	1 jar (170 mL)
1 tbsp.	olive oil	15 mL
	Salt and pepper to taste	
	Mixed greens	
4 oz.	soft goat cheese, crumbled	125 g

1. In a bowl, combine beans, red pepper, onion, artichokes and their marinade and olive oil.
2. Season with salt and pepper.
3. Arrange salad greens on 2 plates; spoon bean salad on top.
4. Garnish with crumbled goat cheese.

Another Bean Salad

~~~~~~~~~~~~~~~~~~~~~~~~~~~~

2 tbsp.	chopped fresh coriander	30 mL
1 tbsp.	chopped fresh parsley	15 mL
1 tbsp.	fresh lime juice	15 mL
¼ tsp.	salt	1 mL
¼ tsp.	pepper	1 mL
1 can (14 oz.)	black beans, rinsed and drained	1 can (398 mL)
1	avocado, diced	1
3 tbsp.	chopped green onion	45 mL
4 cups	mixed salad greens	1 L

1. Combine coriander, parsley, lime juice, salt and pepper.
2. Add beans, avocado and green onions. Cover and chill for 2 hours.
3. Serve over salad greens.

Ensalata Misto

S E R V E S 6

4	tomatoes	4
1	large Spanish onion	1
2	green peppers	2
½ cup	green olives (optional)	125 mL
	Tomato Salad Dressing (below)	

1. Cut tomatoes into wedges and remove seeds. Put in salad bowl.
2. Cut Spanish onion into wedges. Add to bowl.
3. Cut green pepper into strips. Add to bowl.
4. Add olives (if desired) and Tomato Salad Dressing. Toss and serve.

Tomato Salad Dressing

Yields 1¼ cups/300 mL

1 cup	tomato juice	250 mL
2 tbsp.	rice vinegar	30 mL
1 tbsp.	minced onion	15 mL
¼ tsp.	dried basil	1 mL
¼ tsp.	dry mustard	1 mL
1	clove garlic, minced	1
	Salt and pepper to taste	

1. Put all ingredients in a jar and shake well. Chill before serving.

Mixed Green Salad with Curry Dressing

8 cups	mixed salad greens	2 L
1 cup	sliced mushrooms	250 mL
2	tomatoes, diced	2
1	stalk celery, sliced	1
1	small onion, sliced	1
½ cup	diced green pepper	125 mL
	Curry Dressing (below)	

1. Place greens and vegetables in a large salad bowl.
2. Prepare Curry Dressing and pour over salad. Toss.

Curry Dressing

Yields 1⅓ cups/325 mL

½ cup	no-fat sour cream	125 mL
½ cup	skim milk	125 mL
2 tbsp.	white vinegar	30 mL
1 tbsp.	lemon juice	15 mL
2 tsp.	sugar	10 mL
1 tsp.	curry powder	5 mL

1. Blend all ingredients until smooth.

Pickles

Mother's Spiced Tomato Sauce

Perkinsfield Tomato Relish

Mrs. B's Dilled Green Tomatoes

Annie P's Watermelon Rind Pickles

Good Neighbour Pickle

Grannie's Pepper Relish

Jessie's Pickled Beets

Prize-Winning Bread and Butter Pickles

Rhubarb Chutney

Brandied Peaches

Mother's Spiced Tomato Sauce

YIELDS 3 PINTS / 1.5 L

~~~~~~~~~~~~~~~~~~~~~~~~~~~~~

4 lb.	ripe tomatoes, peeled	2 kg
4 cups	brown sugar	1 L
2 cups	white vinegar	500 mL
3	cinnamon sticks	3
1 tbsp.	whole cloves	15 mL

1. Chop tomatoes and place in a large soup pot.
2. Add brown sugar and vinegar.
3. Tie spices in a cheesecloth bag and add to the tomatoes.
4. Stew over low heat for several hours, stirring occasionally. Consistency should be thick. Discard spice bag.
5. Pour into sterilized jars. Store in fridge if using within several weeks. Otherwise, freeze.

Perkinsfield Tomato Relish

20 cups	chopped tomatoes	5 L
8 cups	chopped onions	2 L
4 cups	chopped green peppers	1 L
3 cups	chopped red peppers	750 mL
3 cups	diced celery	750 mL
2 tbsp.	dried chili flakes	30 mL
3 cups	white vinegar	750 mL
2 cups	sugar	500 mL
3 tsp.	salt	15 mL
1 tsp.	each ginger, ground cloves, cinnamon, celery seed, allspice and nutmeg	5 mL
	Pepper to taste	

1. In a large pot, combine all ingredients; bring to a boil.
2. Reduce heat and simmer, uncovered, until thickened, approximately 3 hours. Stir frequently.
3. Fill hot sterilized jars to within ¼ inch (5 mm) of brim. Seal.

Mrs. B's Dilled Green Tomatoes

YIELDS APPROX. 24 PINTS / 12 L

½ bushel	green tomatoes	½ bushel
3 or 4	red peppers	3 or 4
8	garlic bulbs	8
1 or 2	bunches fresh dill	1 or 2
8 cups	water	2 L
4 cups	white vinegar	1 L
¾ cup	coarse salt	175 mL

1. Cut tomatoes into 1-inch (2.5 cm) pieces.
2. Slice red peppers into thin strips.
3. Peel garlic cloves.
4. Cut dill into sprigs.
5. Pack each sterilized jar with green tomatoes, 4 red pepper strips, 4 garlic cloves and 4 dill sprigs.
6. Combine water, vinegar and salt in a large pot and bring to a boil.
7. Fill each jar to within ¼ inch (5 mm) of brim with hot liquid brine; seal immediately.

Annie P's Watermelon Rind Pickles

YIELDS 8 PINTS / 4 L

~~~~~~~~~~~~~~~~~~~~~~~~~~~~~~

	Rind of 1 large watermelon	
¼ cup	pickling salt	50 mL
4 cups	water	1 L
8 cups	sugar	2 L
4 cups	cider vinegar	1 L
2 tbsp.	whole cloves	30 mL
5	cinnamon sticks	5
2 tbsp.	whole allspice	30 mL

1. Remove all red and pink watermelon flesh from the rind.
2. Cut rind into 1-inch (2.5 cm) cubes or slices.
3. Cover and soak overnight in pickling salt and 4 cups (1 L) water.
4. Next day, drain thoroughly. In a large saucepan, cover with fresh cold water and simmer until rind is almost tender. Drain thoroughly.
5. Combine sugar and vinegar in a large kettle. Tie spices in a cheesecloth and add to the pot. Bring to a boil and simmer, uncovered, for 5 minutes.
6. Add drained watermelon rind; simmer for 15 minutes or until rind is clear and translucent.
7. Discard spice bag.
8. Pack rind into sterilized jars. Fill each jar to within ¼ inch (5 mm) of brim with hot brine. Seal immediately.

Preparation Note

Well worth the effort!

Good Neighbour Pickle

YIELDS APPROX. 8 PINTS / 4 L

~~~~~~~~~~~~~~~~~~~~~~~~~~~~~~

9–10	large overripe pickling cucumbers	9–10
5	large onions	5
1	red pepper	1
1	small hot red pepper (optional)	1
½ cup	pickling salt	125 mL
3 cups	sugar	750 mL
2½ cups	white vinegar	625 mL
1 cup	water	250 mL
1 tbsp.	celery seed	15 mL
½ cup	all-purpose flour	125 mL
2 tbsp.	dry mustard	30 mL
1 tsp.	turmeric	5 mL

1. Peel and thinly slice cucumbers and onions.
2. Thinly slice red pepper and hot pepper. Place all vegetables in a large nonreactive container and toss with the pickling salt.
3. Let stand overnight. The next morning drain the vegetables.
4. Combine sugar, vinegar, water and celery seed in a large kettle. Add drained vegetables.
5. Bring vegetables and brine to a boil, making sure sugar dissolves completely.
6. Mix flour, dry mustard and turmeric with enough of the brine to make a lump-free paste. Add to the pot and stir until thickened.
7. Fill hot sterilized pickle jars to within ¼ inch (5 mm) of brim. Seal.

Preparation Note

This is a good way to use up large overripe cucumbers.

Grannie's Pepper Relish

YIELDS 10 PINTS / 5 L

12	green peppers, finely chopped	12
12	red peppers, finely chopped	12
5 cups	sugar	1.25 L
4 cups	white vinegar	1 L
3 tbsp.	pickling salt	45 mL
1 tbsp.	mustard seed	15 mL

1. Place peppers in a large bowl and cover with boiling water. Let stand 15 minutes. Drain well.
2. Place peppers in a large kettle. Add sugar, vinegar, salt and mustard seed. Boil until tender.
3. Fill sterilized jars to within ¼ inch (5 mm) of brim. Seal.

Preparation Note

This recipe can be halved or quartered.

Jessie's Pickled Beets

YIELDS 2–3 PINTS / 1–1.5 L

1½ lb.	small beets	750 g
1 tbsp.	pickling spice	15 mL
1½ cups	cider vinegar	375 mL
1 cup	brown sugar	250 mL
½ cup	water	125 mL

1. Boil beets until tender. Drain; when cool enough to handle, rub off skins, and slice or leave whole.
2. Pack in hot sterilized jars.
3. Tie pickling spice in a cheesecloth bag.
4. Combine the spice bag, vinegar, sugar and water. Bring to a boil for 5 minutes. Remove spice bag. Pour boiling liquid over beets to within ¼ inch (5 mm) of brim. Seal immediately.

Prize-Winning Bread and Butter Pickles

25	pickling cucumbers, 1–1½ inches (2.5–4 cm) in diameter	25
8	large onions	8
½ cup	coarse salt	125 mL
5 cups	sugar	1.25 L
5 cups	cider vinegar	1.25 L
2 tbsp.	mustard seed	30 mL
2 tbsp.	celery seed	30 mL
2 tbsp.	turmeric	30 mL
½ tsp.	ground cloves	2 mL

1. Scrub cucumbers and slice thinly. Do not peel.
2. Cut onion into thin slices; combine with cucumbers and salt in a large bowl.
3. Let stand, covered, at room temperature for 3 hours. Drain well.
4. Combine remaining ingredients in a large pot and bring to a boil. Add drained cucumbers and onions; bring to a boil for 1 minute.
5. Fill sterilized jars to within ¼ inch (5 mm) of brim. Seal.

Rhubarb Chutney

YIELDS 2–2½ PINTS / 1–1.25 L

1 tbsp.	pickling spice	15 mL
7 cups	½-inch (1 cm) pieces rhubarb	1.75 L
1	large onion, sliced	1
2 cups	brown sugar	500 mL
1 cup	cider vinegar	250 mL
1 tsp.	cinnamon	5 mL
1 tsp.	ginger	5 mL
¾ tsp.	salt	4 mL
½ tsp.	allspice	2 mL
½ tsp.	ground cloves	2 mL
1 cup	raisins	250 mL

1. Tie pickling spice in a piece of cheesecloth.
2. Combine rhubarb, onion, sugar, vinegar and other spices in a large kettle. Add the pickling spice. Simmer, uncovered, for 20 minutes, stirring often.
3. Add raisins and cook for another 20 minutes, stirring to prevent sticking.
4. Pour into sterilized jars to within ¼ inch (5 mm) of brim. Seal.

Serving Suggestion

Serve with curries.

Brandied Peaches

YIELDS 7 PINTS / 3.5 L

~~~~~~

6 lb.	small peaches	3 kg
12 cups	sugar	3 L
5 ¼ cups	water	1.25 L
3 cups	brandy	750 mL

1. Peel, pit and halve peaches.
2. Combine sugar and water in a large pot. Bring to a boil, stirring to dissolve sugar. Boil 5 minutes. Reduce to a simmer.
3. Place 1 layer of peaches at a time in the boiling syrup and simmer slowly, about 5 minutes, until peaches are tender.
4. Remove peaches with a slotted spoon and pack into sterilized jars.
5. Boil syrup 5 more minutes, remove from heat and stir in brandy. Pour syrup over fruit in jars to within ¼ inch (5 mm) of brim. Seal.
6. Store in a cool, dark place for at least 2 weeks before serving.

Serving Suggestion

A quick and elegant dessert to have on hand.

5
Fall

~~~~~~~~~~~~~~~~~~~~~~~~

The Kids Are Gone

Dinner Bridge

Autumn Splendour

Harvest Get-Together

Crazy Eights

After the Game

Fall Affair

Rakers' Reward

Four for Fall

Georgian Bay Bounty

Masquerade Dinner

*P*ICTURE A GROUP OF SEVEN PORTRAIT of a Georgian Bay forest in autumn, bathed in evening pastels, the forest trails carpeted with soft yellow leaves, the canopy ablaze in red and gold. The western sky is awash in soft blue, pink and grey tones. This is the wondrously tranquil fall scene that usually awaits the onslaught of the Huronia Hash House Harriers.

The Harriers have become a local icon. They play a modified game of Paper Chase, or Hares and Hounds, running and walking weekly through some of Huronia's scenic areas. We diligently try to live up to the group motto, "Terminally Immature," and after ten years of weekly adventures, if no longer young, we remain young at heart. The fun continues at the traditional after-run celebration called the "on-on," where food and refreshments are served and many of the group are showered with lighthearted abuse.

The fall colours call out to the outdoor enthusiast around Georgian Bay, but autumn is also a time when we take in the peace and quiet of summer's aftermath. The tourists have all left, and the kids have gone back to school or to far-off places of employment. There is less traffic on the Bay, and nothing more beautiful than the sight of a single sailboat slipping across the water against the glorious shoreline colour. Backyard barbecues for casts of thousands are replaced by quiet dinners for two, and we all seem to lie in wait for the onslaught of the Georgian Bay winter.

As time marches on, we appreciate the simple pleasures in life more and more, and our remarkable Georgian Bay seasons provide the settings. Recently a friend celebrated her fiftieth birthday in the fall by hiking up to McCrae Lake with a group of twenty good friends. The trek took several hours, but it was a beautiful autumn afternoon. When they made camp near the lake, a feast of treats for all the hungry hikers came from one single knapsack. When the feast was over and they had basked in the warmth and spirit of friendship on a truly spectacular fall afternoon, they all hiked back to town. It was a simple event, but our friend remarked that it was the most wonderful way to turn fifty years of age.

The fall line-up of fresh fruits and vegetables lends itself to diverse taste sensations. Apples, tomatoes, squash, carrots, turnips, beets and cabbage, to name a few, have been used in our fall menus without all the cream sauces and cheeses we once thought we needed. Herbs and broth, skim milk and no-fat sour cream combined with this wonderful bounty still make for some delicious meals.

Try our The Kids Are Gone menu as a special treat after transporting "them" back to school and topping up their bank accounts! The Harvest Get-Together is a wonderful choice for a different kind of Thanksgiving dinner, and our hearty Rakers' Reward menu is just that!

The docks are out, the boats are stored. We're ready for our Georgian Bay winter, eh!

The Kids Are Gone

FOR 2

Shrimp and Mango Salad

Fettuccine with Tomatoes,
Prosciutto and Basil

Peasant Bread

Baked Apples

Shrimp and Mango Salad

SERVES 2

~~~~~~~~~~~~~~~~~~~~~~~~~~~~~~

2	mangoes	2
	Horseradish Dressing (below)	
8	large shrimp, peeled, deveined and cooked	8
4	large lettuce leaves	4
1	red pepper, cut into strips	1
	Fresh mint leaves	

1. Peel mangoes and cut flesh in cubes.
2. Prepare Horseradish Dressing.
3. Cut shrimp into chunks; combine with mango and dressing.
4. Place 2 lettuce leaves on each salad plate and arrange mango-shrimp mixture on top.
5. Broil pepper strips on a baking sheet until golden brown.
6. Garnish salads with red pepper and mint leaves. Chill until serving time.

Horseradish Dressing

Yields ⅔ cup/150 mL

1 tbsp.	prepared horseradish	15 mL
½ cup	light mayonnaise	125 mL
½ tsp.	sugar	2 mL
½ tsp.	lemon juice	2 mL
	Freshly ground pepper	

1. Put all ingredients in a jar and shake well.

Fettuccine with Tomatoes, Prosciutto and Basil

SERVES 2

3	medium tomatoes	3
4 oz.	thinly sliced prosciutto, cut into ½-inch (1 cm) strips	125 g
½ cup	chopped fresh basil	125 mL
3 tbsp.	olive oil	45 mL
1 tbsp.	balsamic vinegar	15 mL
2	large cloves garlic, minced	2
	Salt and cracked black pepper to taste	
8 oz.	fettuccine	250 g
2 tbsp.	grated Parmesan cheese	30 mL

1. Remove seeds and pulp from tomatoes. Chop tomatoes.
2. Mix tomatoes, prosciutto, basil, olive oil, vinegar and garlic in a large bowl.
3. Season with salt and cracked pepper.
4. Cook fettuccine and drain.
5. Toss hot pasta with tomato mixture; top with Parmesan.
6. Serve immediately!

Preparation Note

Steps 1, 2 and 3 can be done well ahead of time, and the tomato mixture kept chilled until ready to use.

Peasant Bread

―――――――――――――――――――――

3 tbsp.	chopped mixed fresh herbs (chives, parsley, basil, marjoram)	45 mL
2 tbsp.	olive oil	30 mL
4	slices dense crusty bread, ½-inch (1 cm) thick	4
2 tbsp.	grated light Parmesan cheese	30 mL

1. Combine herbs and oil in a small bowl. Let stand 15 minutes.
2. Preheat broiler.
3. Place bread on a baking sheet; brush bread with half of the herb oil.
4. Broil until bread is just beginning to colour. Watch closely.
5. Turn bread over and brush with remaining herb oil.
6. Sprinkle bread with Parmesan cheese. Broil until cheese topping is browned. Watch closely as bread will burn easily.
7. Serve immediately.

Baked Apples

(Microwave)

2	apples	2
2 tbsp.	raisins	30 mL
¼ cup	brown sugar or maple syrup	50 mL
	Cinnamon	
	Nutmeg	
¼ cup	apple juice	50 mL

1. Core apples and stand in a microwave-safe bowl.
2. Spoon raisins into apples and top with brown sugar or syrup.
3. Sprinkle with cinnamon and nutmeg; drizzle apple juice over top.
4. Cover dish with vented plastic wrap. Microwave on High for 2 to 4 minutes, being careful not to overcook. Let stand for 10 minutes.
5. Transfer apples to serving bowls and spoon pan juices over apples.

Serving Suggestion

Serve with vanilla yogurt.

Dinner Bridge

FOR 8

Leafy Strawberry Salad

No-Trump Chicken

Sautéed Potatoes

Sweet-and-Sour Brussels Sprouts

Peachy Keen

Leafy Strawberry Salad

SERVES 8

1	bunch leaf lettuce	1
2 cups	mixed salad greens	500 mL
2 cups	sliced strawberries	500 mL
1	small red onion, sliced in rings	1
½ cup	sliced celery	125 mL
½ cup	toasted slivered almonds	125 mL
	Raspberry Vinaigrette (page 48)	

1. Tear lettuce leaves; combine with mixed salad greens in a large salad bowl.
2. Add sliced strawberries, onion and celery.
3. When ready to serve, top with toasted almonds and vinaigrette. Toss.

No-Trump Chicken

SERVES 8

Oven: 350°F/180°C

¾ cup	no-fat yogurt	175 mL
4 tbsp.	Dijon mustard	60 mL
1½ cups	crushed bran flakes	375 mL
1 tbsp.	dried thyme	15 mL
1 tsp.	dried basil	5 mL
1 tsp.	dried oregano	5 mL
	Salt and pepper	
8	boneless, skinless chicken breasts	8

1. Spray a baking sheet with cooking spray.
2. Mix yogurt and mustard together.
3. In a shallow dish, mix crushed bran flakes and herbs.
4. Sprinkle salt and pepper over the chicken. Dip chicken in yogurt mixture.
5. Dip chicken in bran flake mixture. Arrange on baking sheet.
6. Bake for 40 minutes or until chicken is no longer pink inside.

Serving Suggestion

Serve with **Mother's Spiced Tomato Sauce** (page 168).

Sautéed Potatoes

10	potatoes, peeled	10
1 tsp.	salt	5 mL
2 tsp.	sugar	10 mL
¼ cup	vegetable broth	50 mL
2 tsp.	canola oil	10 mL
	Chopped fresh parsley	

1. Quarter potatoes and place in boiling water with salt and sugar. Cover and boil until tender. Drain.
2. In a large saucepan over medium heat, heat broth and oil. Sauté potatoes until slightly brown, stirring frequently.
3. Sprinkle with parsley and serve.

Sweet-and-Sour Brussels Sprouts

SERVES 8

~~~~~~~~~~~~~~~~~~~~

4 cups	Brussels sprouts	1 L
2 tbsp.	wine vinegar	30 mL
1 tbsp.	olive oil	15 mL
¼ cup	vegetable broth	50 mL
1 tsp.	cornstarch	5 mL
1 tbsp.	honey	15 mL
2 tsp.	sugar	10 mL
1	clove garlic, minced	1
½ tsp.	salt	2 mL
	Pepper to taste	
1 tbsp.	vegetable bacon bits	15 mL

1. Steam sprouts for 10 minutes or until slightly tender. Drain.
2. Blend vinegar and olive oil; heat in a small saucepan.
3. Blend vegetable broth and cornstarch; add to the oil and vinegar. Stir until thickened.
4. Add honey, sugar, garlic, salt and pepper. Stir well.
5. Add sauce to sprouts and toss until well coated and heated through.
6. Garnish with vegetable bacon bits.

Peachy Keen

SERVES 8

Oven: 375°F/190°C

5 cups	sliced peaches	1.25 L
¾ cup	brown sugar	175 mL
¾ cup	oats	175 mL
4 tbsp.	all-purpose flour	60 mL
4 tbsp.	light butter	60 mL
¾ cup	chopped almonds	175 mL
2 tbsp.	applesauce	30 mL

1. Place peaches in a lightly sprayed 8 cup (2 L) baking dish.
2. Mix sugar, oats and flour in a large bowl.
3. Cut butter into pieces and, with a pastry blender, cut butter into the oat mixture until it looks like coarse meal.
4. Stir almonds and applesauce into crumble mixture; pour over the peaches.
5. Bake for 40 minutes or until brown and bubbly.

Autumn Splendour

FOR 4

Waldorf Salad

Filet Mignon with Peppercorn Mustard Sauce

"Where's the Garlic?" Potatoes

Roasted Fennel and Onions

Maple Carrots

Cantaloupe Cups

Poppyseed Cake

Waldorf Salad

~~~~~~~~~~~~~~~~~~~~~~~~~~~~~~~~~~~~~~~

2 cups	diced apples	500 mL
2 tbsp.	lemon juice	30 mL
1 tsp.	liquid honey	5 mL
1¼ cups	diced celery	300 mL
½ cup	light or no-fat mayonnaise	125 mL
	Pinch nutmeg	
½ cup	walnut halves	125 mL
	Lettuce leaves	

1. In a bowl, toss apples with lemon juice and honey.
2. Add celery and toss.
3. Spoon in the mayonnaise and flavour with nutmeg. Toss.
4. When ready to serve, add the walnuts and serve on a bed of lettuce.

Filet Mignon with Peppercorn Mustard Sauce

SERVES 4

4	beef filets (4 oz./125 g each)	4
	Salt and freshly ground pepper	
1 tsp.	olive oil	5 mL
½ cup	minced shallots	125 mL
½ cup	cognac	125 mL
½ cup	beef broth	125 mL
¼ cup	green peppercorn mustard	50 mL

1. Sprinkle filets with salt and pepper.
2. Heat oil in cast iron frying pan or heavy skillet on medium-high heat until hot.
3. Add steaks; cook 5 minutes each side or until done to your taste.
4. Remove steaks from skillet; keep them warm.
5. Add shallots to pan and sauté 30 seconds.
6. Add cognac and cook 10 seconds.
7. Add broth and mustard. Stir well.
8. Reduce heat and cook 2 minutes, stirring constantly.
9. Serve sauce over steaks.

"Where's the Garlic?" Potatoes

SERVES 4

Oven: 400°F/200°C

4	large potatoes	4
2 tbsp.	olive oil	30 mL
2 tsp.	chopped fresh basil	10 mL
	Freshly ground black pepper	
4	cloves garlic, peeled and halved	4

1. Using an apple corer, carefully remove a ½-inch (1 cm) plug from each potato, making sure not to go right through potato. Cut off two-thirds of each plug and discard, keeping "cap."
2. Combine oil, basil and pepper.
3. Fill each potato hole with 2 garlic halves and one-quarter of the basil mixture.
4. Replace "caps" in each hole.
5. Bake on a baking sheet for 1 hour, or until potatoes are tender.

Preparation Note

This dish can also be cooked on the barbecue. Follow steps 1 through 4; then wrap each potato in foil.

Potatoes are a rich source of vitamin C, not the fatty food we think. The fat comes from the method of cooking or the toppings. Use no-fat sour cream, low-fat sour cream or yogurt instead.

Roasted Fennel and Onions

~~~~~~~~~~~~~~~~~~~~~~~~~~~~~~~~~

Oven: 400°F/200°C

2	fennel bulbs	2
5	medium onions, peeled and quartered	5
2 tbsp.	olive oil	30 mL
½ cup	balsamic vinegar	125 mL
	Freshly ground black pepper	

1. Remove root end and fronds from fennel bulbs; core and cut into wedges.
2. Place onions and fennel in oiled baking dish and toss with oil, vinegar and pepper.
3. Bake 1 hour.
4. Serve immediately.

Fennel is low in calories and rich in vitamin A, calcium and potassium.

Maple Carrots

~~~~~~~~~~~~~~~~~~~~~~~~~~~~~~~~~~~~~~~

1 lb.	carrots, peeled and julienned	500 g
2 tbsp.	maple syrup	30 mL
1 tsp.	lemon zest	5 mL

1. Steam carrots until tender. Drain.
2. Drizzle maple syrup over carrots and add zest. Stir until well coated. Serve.

Cantaloupe Cups

~~~~~~~~~~~~~~~~~~~~~~~~~~~~~~~~

½ cup	no-fat plain yogurt	125 mL
2–3 tbsp.	maple syrup	30–45 mL
2	small cantaloupes	2
4 cups	mixed fruit	1 L

1. Blend yogurt and maple syrup. Refrigerate until ready to serve.
2. Cut cantaloupes in half. Remove seeds and cut melon balls out of the fruit. Keep the shells for serving bowls.
3. In a bowl, combine the melon with fruit of your choice. Try bananas, mandarins, lychee fruit, pineapple, mangoes.
4. Spoon fruit into the cantaloupe shells. Top each with a spoonful or two of the sweetened yogurt.

Poppyseed Cake

YIELDS 1 BUNDT CAKE

Oven: 350°F/180°C

¾ cup	poppyseeds	175 mL
1¼ cups	1% milk	300 mL
½ cup	light butter	125 mL
1½ cups	sugar	375 mL
1 tsp.	vanilla	5 mL
4	egg whites	4
3 tsp.	baking powder	15 mL
2½ cups	all-purpose flour	625 mL

1. Soak the poppyseeds in milk; set aside.
2. In a large bowl, cream butter and sugar until fluffy. Stir in vanilla.
3. In a separate bowl, beat egg whites until stiff.
4. Fold egg whites and poppyseeds into the butter and sugar.
5. Add baking powder and flour, stirring just to combine. Pour batter into an 8-cup (2 L) bundt pan coated with cooking spray.
6. Bake for 1 hour or until golden and firm to touch. Cool 10 minutes in pan and turn out onto rack.

Harvest Get-Together

FOR 8

Light Broccoli Soup

Pork Tenderloin in Honey-Apple Marinade

Orange Sweet Potatoes

Baked Tomatoes with Creamed Spinach

Applesauce-Orange Spice Cake

Light Broccoli Soup

~~~~~~~~~~~~~~~~~~~~~~~~~~~~~~~~~

1	large onion, chopped	1
2	cloves garlic, minced	2
2	bunches broccoli, coarsely chopped	2
1½ cups	chopped celery	375 mL
6 cups	chicken broth	1.5 L
⅓ cup	skim milk powder	75 mL
	Salt and pepper to taste	
	Dash hot pepper sauce (optional)	

1. Place onion, garlic, broccoli, celery and chicken broth in a large saucepan. Simmer for 15 to 20 minutes or until broccoli is tender.
2. In a food processor or blender, purée the soup in batches until smooth. Add skim milk powder to the last batch; blend until powder is dissolved.
3. Return soup to saucepan over low heat; season with salt and pepper.
4. Add hot pepper sauce and serve.

Preparation Note

Vegetable broth can be substituted for the chicken broth.

Pork Tenderloin in Honey-Apple Marinade

SERVES 8

Oven: 350°F/180°C

1 cup	apple juice	250 mL
⅔ cup	liquid honey	150 mL
3 tbsp.	soy sauce	45 mL
2 tbsp.	minced garlic	30 mL
2 tbsp.	grated fresh ginger	30 mL
2 tbsp.	canola oil	30 mL
1 tbsp.	honey mustard	15 mL
6	green onions, chopped	6
1 tsp.	pepper	5 mL
3 lb.	pork tenderloin	1.5 kg
4	apples, peeled, cored and cut in wedges	4
1 tbsp.	lemon juice	15 mL
1 tbsp.	margarine	15 mL

1. In a large, resealable plastic bag, combine apple juice, ½ cup (125 mL) of the honey, soy sauce, garlic, ginger, oil, honey mustard, green onions and pepper.
2. Add the pork tenderloins and seal tightly. Place bag in a large container and refrigerate overnight (or at least 6 hours). Turn bag several times.

3. Remove pork from bag; save the marinade.
4. Place pork in an oiled large, shallow baking dish. Pour half the marinade over the meat.
5. Bake for 1 hour, basting often with remaining marinade. Let stand, covered, for 15 minutes. Do not turn off oven.
6. Meanwhile, in a large bowl, toss apple wedges with lemon juice.
7. Melt margarine; stir in remaining 2 tbsp. (30 mL) of the honey. Pour over apples and toss.
8. Place coated apples on a cookie sheet; bake for 15 minutes or until soft.
9. Slice pork into 1-inch (2.5 cm) slices. Arrange on warm serving platter. Spoon apples over pork slices and serve.

Orange Sweet Potatoes

~~~~~~~~~~~~~~~~~~~~~~~~

Oven: 350°F/180°C

4	large sweet potatoes	4
⅓ cup	orange juice	75 mL
¼ tsp.	orange zest	1 mL
	Pinch salt	
2 tbsp.	brown sugar	30 mL

1. Bake sweet potatoes in their skins for 45 minutes or until tender. (Or cut into chunks and microwave for approximately 12 minutes.)
2. Let potatoes cool. Skin and mash.
3. Stir in orange juice, zest and salt. Place mixture in a 7- x 11-inch (2 L) casserole dish. Sprinkle with brown sugar.
4. Cover and bake for 30 minutes. Remove cover and continue baking for 15 minutes.

Baked Tomatoes with Creamed Spinach

SERVES 8

~~~~~~~~~~~~~~~~~~~~~~~

Oven: 350°F/180°C

8	medium tomatoes	8
	Salt	
2 lb.	spinach	1 kg
8 tbsp.	vegetable broth	125 mL
2 tbsp.	all-purpose flour	30 mL
1½ cups	milk	375 mL
	Salt and pepper to taste	
½ tsp.	nutmeg (or to taste)	2 mL

1. Core tomatoes, removing tops and seeds but leaving thick shells.
2. Sprinkle with salt. Invert on a wire rack; let stand for 1 hour.
3. Steam spinach for 5 minutes or until wilted. Rinse with cold water, drain well and chop finely.
4. In a medium saucepan over medium heat, heat spinach and 4 tbsp. (60 mL) vegetable broth for 3 minutes.
5. In a separate saucepan, whisk together flour and remaining 4 tbsp. (60 mL) vegetable broth over medium heat for 3 minutes. Slowly stir in milk and continue to cook until smooth and thickened.
6. Add white sauce to spinach; simmer for 10 minutes.
7. Season with salt, pepper and nutmeg to taste.
8. Purée mixture and fill tomatoes.
9. Bake for 15 minutes in an ovenproof dish. Serve immediately.

Applesauce-Orange Spice Cake

SERVES 8

Oven: 350°F/180°C

1½ cups	unsweetened applesauce	375 mL
½ cup	sugar	125 mL
3 tbsp.	orange juice	45 mL
2 tbsp.	olive oil	30 mL
2	egg whites	2
2 tsp.	grated orange zest	10 mL
1½ tsp.	orange extract	7 mL
1 tsp.	vanilla	5 mL
1¼ cups	all-purpose flour	300 mL
1 cup	whole-wheat flour	250 mL
1¼ tsp.	cinnamon	6 mL
1 tsp.	baking powder	5 mL
1 tsp.	baking soda	5 mL
¼ tsp.	ground cloves	1 mL
½ cup	raisins	125 mL
2 tsp.	sugar	10 mL
½ tsp.	cinnamon	2 mL

1. Spray an 8-cup (2 L) bundt pan with cooking spray.
2. In a large bowl, place applesauce, ½ cup (125 mL) sugar, orange juice, oil, egg whites, orange zest, orange extract and vanilla. Mix well.

3. Combine flours, 1¼ tsp. (6 mL) cinnamon, baking powder, baking soda, cloves and raisins. Add to liquid ingredients; stir well.
4. Spoon batter into prepared pan. Combine 2 tsp. (10 mL) sugar and ½ tsp. (2 mL) cinnamon; sprinkle over cake batter.
5. Bake for 35 minutes or until firm to touch.
6. Cool in pan for 5 minutes and remove to rack to cool.

Crazy Eights

FOR 8

Coriander Black Bean Dip

Pita Crisps

Spicy Tomato and Tofu with Pasta

Sunshine Spinach Salad

Reduced Great Brown Bread

Very Berry Angel Food Cake

Coriander Black Bean Dip

YIELDS 2 CUPS / 500 ML

¼ cup	water	50 mL
½ cup	chopped onion	125 mL
5	cloves garlic, minced	5
1 can (14 oz.)	black beans, drained and rinsed	1 can (398 mL)
½ tsp.	ground cumin	2 mL
1 tbsp.	minced jalapeno pepper (or to taste) (optional)	15 mL
⅓ cup	mild salsa	75 mL
⅓ cup	chopped fresh coriander	75 mL
	Salt and pepper to taste	

1. Heat water in a nonstick frying pan; sauté onion and garlic for 2 to 3 minutes.
2. Mash beans and add to onion and garlic mixture. Add cumin, jalapeno pepper (if desired) and salsa.
3. Cook for 5 minutes, stirring occasionally. Add a little more water if necessary.
4. Remove from heat. Stir in coriander, salt and pepper.
5. Serve with pita pieces, vegetables or fat-free tortilla chips.

Pita Crisps

~~~~~~

Oven: 275°F/140°C

2	pita breads	2
¼ cup	olive oil	50 mL
1	clove garlic, crushed	1

1. Cut each pita bread into 6 wedges, and then cut open so you have 24 pieces.
2. Combine oil and garlic. Let stand for 15 minutes.
3. Lay wedges on a large cookie sheet. Brush each with a little garlic oil.
4. Bake for 10 minutes. Turn crisps and brush again with a bit of oil. Return to oven for 10 more minutes or until crisp. Remove from oven and cool. Store in a sealed plastic bag.

Preparation Note

Bagels can be used for this recipe. Slice them thinly and brush with oil and garlic. They may take longer than pitas to dry out and become crisp.

Serving Suggestion

Serve with dip—for example, hummus or bean dip—or eat plain.

Spicy Tomato and Tofu with Pasta

SERVES 8

2 tbsp.	vegetable broth	30 mL
1 tsp.	olive oil	5 mL
1	large onion, chopped	1
4	cloves garlic, pressed	4
1 cup	chopped green pepper	250 mL
½ cup	chopped celery	125 mL
12 oz.	soft tofu, cut in small cubes	375 g
½ lb.	sliced mushrooms	250 g
2 cans (28 oz.)	tomatoes, chopped	2 cans (796 mL)
1 tbsp.	paprika	15 mL
3	bay leaves	3
	Salt and pepper to taste	
	Angel hair pasta	

1. Heat broth and oil in a large frying pan over medium heat.
2. Add onion, garlic, pepper, celery, tofu and mushrooms. Reduce heat to medium-low and cook for 5 minutes, stirring occasionally.
3. Add tomatoes, paprika, bay leaves, salt and pepper. Reduce heat to low and cook for 20 minutes. Discard bay leaves.
4. Cook pasta until tender. Add to tomato mixture and mix well. Serve immediately.

Sunshine Spinach Salad

SERVES 8

2 packages (10 oz)	fresh spinach, trimmed	2 packages (284 g)
1 can (10 oz.)	mandarin oranges, drained (reserve juice)	1 can (284 mL)
1	small onion, sliced in rings	1
	Orange Vinegar Dressing (below)	

1. Tear spinach leaves and place in salad bowl.
2. Toss spinach with orange pieces and onion rings.
3. Add dressing and toss to coat.

Orange Vinegar Dressing

Yields ½ cup/125 mL

2 tbsp.	rice vinegar	30 mL
½ tsp.	Dijon mustard	2 mL
2	cloves garlic, minced	2
1½ tsp.	olive oil	7 mL
2 tbsp.	water	30 mL
3 tbsp.	orange juice	45 mL

1. Shake all ingredients in a jar. Chill.

Reduced Great Brown Bread

YIELDS 1 LOAF

~~~~~~~~~~~~~~~~~~~~

Oven: 350°F/180°C

1½ cups	bran flakes	375 mL
1 cup	skim milk	250 mL
2 cups	all-purpose flour	500 mL
⅔ cup	sugar	150 mL
2 tsp.	baking powder	10 mL
¾ tsp.	salt	4 mL
¼ tsp.	baking soda	1 mL
¾ cup	unsweetened applesauce	175 mL
2 tbsp.	molasses	30 mL
2	egg whites	2

1. Soften bran flakes in milk.
2. Sift together dry ingredients.
3. In a large bowl, mix the applesauce, molasses and egg whites. Mix in the softened bran flakes and milk.
4. Add the dry ingredients and stir to moisten.
5. Pour into a greased 9- x 5-inch (2 L) loaf pan. Bake for 1 hour or until tester comes out clean.
6. Cool in pan for 10 minutes; then turn out onto a cooling rack.

Very Berry Angel Food Cake

Oven: 325°F/160°C

2 cups	egg whites (16 eggs)	500 mL
¼ tsp.	salt	1 mL
1 tsp.	cream of tartar	5 mL
½ tsp.	almond extract	2 mL
1 tsp.	vanilla	5 mL
1¼ cups	fruit sugar	300 mL
1 cup	cake flour	250 mL
	Frozen raspberries, strawberries and blueberries	

1. Prepare a 9-inch (3 L) tube pan by dusting with flour.
2. Beat egg whites with salt until foamy; then add cream of tartar and beat until stiff peaks form.
3. Gently add the almond extract and vanilla.
4. Sift the sugar and flour together. Carefully fold into the whites a little at a time until flour mixture is evenly mixed into the whites.

5. Pour batter into tube pan. Bake for 50 minutes or until tester comes out clean. Let stand 10 minutes and then invert pan to cool.
6. Serve with a mixture of fruits.

Preparation Note

Angel food cakes are best made a day ahead. Do not butter or grease the tube pan.

Serving Suggestion

Use fresh fruit if in season.

After the Game

FOR 6

Veggie Shepherd's Pie

Savoury Corn-Filled Tomatoes

(Bread)

Janine's Chocolate Macaroons

Cappuccino

Veggie Shepherd's Pie

SERVES 6

Oven: 350°F/180°C

8	large potatoes	8
½ cup	skim milk	125 mL
2 tbsp.	well-beaten egg whites	30 mL
½ tsp.	salt	2 mL
2 cups	vegetable broth	500 mL
1	medium onion, finely chopped	1
1 tbsp.	Worcestershire sauce	15 mL
2	cloves garlic, finely chopped	2
½ tsp.	dried thyme	2 mL
	Salt and pepper to taste	
2 tbsp.	all-purpose flour	30 mL
1 lb.	Soya Veggie Ground Round	500 g
	Parmesan cheese (optional)	

1. Boil potatoes until tender. Drain.
2. Mash potatoes. Add milk, egg whites and salt. Set aside.
3. In a saucepan, bring broth to a boil. Add onion, Worcestershire sauce, garlic, thyme, salt and pepper. Continue to boil for 3 minutes.
4. Combine flour with a little water; stir into broth to thicken.
5. Add the Veggie Ground Round; heat through. Pour into a 9- x 13-inch (3.5 L) casserole dish.

(continued)

6. Spoon potato mixture on top of casserole. Sprinkle with Parmesan cheese.
7. Bake for 30 minutes or until bubbling. Let stand for 10 minutes before serving.

Preparation Note

There are a variety of soya meat substitutes. Readily available is TVP (textured vegetable protein) in fine or coarse varieties to add to spaghetti sauces, soups and so on. It is an excellent source of protein. Also available are Yves products, such as Veggie Ground Round, which we recommend for this recipe.

Savoury Corn-Filled Tomatoes

SERVES 6

~~~~~~~~~~~~~~~~~~~~~~~~~~~~~~~

Oven: 350°F/180°C

6	tomatoes	6
2 cups	diced mushrooms	500 mL
1 cup	corn kernels	250 mL
½ cup	diced onions	125 mL
1 tsp.	dried dillweed	5 mL
1 tbsp.	olive oil	15 mL
1 tbsp.	lemon juice	15 mL
2 tsp.	Worcestershire sauce	10 mL
2	cloves garlic, minced	2
1½ tsp.	dried basil	7 mL
¼ tsp.	paprika	1 mL
¼ tsp.	salt	1 mL

1. Cut tops off tomatoes and scoop out pulp and seeds to form shells.
2. Combine mushrooms, corn, onions and dill.
3. In a measuring cup or small bowl, combine the oil, lemon juice, Worcestershire sauce, garlic, basil, paprika and salt. Beat lightly with a whisk. Pour dressing over the corn mixture and toss gently.
4. Spoon corn mixture into tomato shells. Bake in a nonstick pan for 20 minutes.

Serving Suggestion

Irish Soda Bread (page 286) complements this menu.

Janine's Chocolate Macaroons

YIELDS 20 COOKIES

¼ cup	1% milk	50 mL
¼ cup	no-fat yogurt	50 mL
4 tbsp.	cocoa	60 mL
¾ cup	sugar	175 mL
1 tbsp.	light butter	15 mL
1 tsp.	vanilla	5 mL
1 ½ cups	oats	375 mL
½ cup	unsweetened shredded coconut	125 mL

1. Combine milk, yogurt, cocoa, sugar and butter in a saucepan. Bring to a boil over medium heat. Boil slowly for 8 to 10 minutes, stirring frequently. Do a soft-ball stage test by dropping 1 tbsp. (15 mL) hot mixture into ¼ cup (50 mL) of cold water. It should form a ball readily.
2. Remove mixture from heat. Add vanilla, oats and coconut. Stir until well combined.
3. Drop by rounded teaspoons onto a cookie sheet. Chill. Keep in an airtight container.

Cappuccino

~~~~~~~~~~~~~~~~~~~~~~~~~~~~~~~~~~~~~~

½ cup	1% milk	125 mL
1	pot espresso or other strong coffee	1
	Pinch cinnamon or cocoa	

1. Put milk in a milk frother and pump until light and frothy.
2. Pour coffee into mugs. Top each with froth.
3. Sprinkle with cinnamon or cocoa.

Preparation Note

A cappuccino maker can be used.

Fall Affair

FOR 6

Citrus-Mango Salad

Tomato-Basil Bread

Veal with Lemon-Caper Sauce

Garlic Green Beans

Mushroom Couscous

Apple-Cranberry Bread Pudding

Citrus-Mango Salad

~~~~~~~~~~~~~~~~~~~~~~~~~~~~~

(Microwave)

1 cup	snow peas (approximately 24)	250 mL
6 cups	mixed salad greens	1.5 L
1 cup	bean sprouts	250 mL
6	mushrooms, thinly sliced	6
½	medium red onion, sliced into rings	½
½	cucumber, peeled and sliced	½
2	carrots, peeled into curls	2
1	medium red pepper, sliced into thin strips	1
12	cherry tomatoes, halved	12
1	orange, peeled and chopped into small pieces	1
1	mango, peeled and sliced lengthwise	1
	Gourmet Salad Dressing (page 226)	
⅓ cup	slivered almonds	75 mL
¼ cup	chopped fresh coriander	50 mL

1. Cook snow peas on High in microwave for 1 minute. Chill until ready to use.
2. Arrange greens on 6 individual salad plates, in a large salad bowl or on a serving platter.

(continued)

225

3. Arrange chilled snow peas and bean sprouts over greens. Follow with the remaining vegetables and fruits.
4. Pour Gourmet Salad Dressing over salad.
5. Garnish with slivered almonds and fresh coriander. Serve immediately.

Gourmet Salad Dressing

Yields 1 cup/250 mL

½ cup	orange juice	125 mL
¼ cup	olive oil	50 mL
3 tbsp.	rice vinegar	45 mL
1 tbsp.	minced garlic	15 mL
1 tbsp.	grated fresh ginger	15 mL
1 tbsp.	soy sauce	15 mL
1 tbsp.	sesame oil	15 mL
1 tsp.	honey mustard	5 mL

1. Whisk all ingredients together. Chill until ready to use.

Preparation Note

Take advantage of the many colours in this salad and be creative when arranging it.

Tomato-Basil Bread

YIELDS 1 LOAF

~~~~~~~~~~~~~~~~~~~~~~~~~~~~~~~~~~~~~

Oven: 325°F/160°C

½ cup	unsweetened applesauce	125 mL
½ cup	egg substitute (or 2 eggs)	125 mL
¼ cup	tomato paste	50 mL
1 tbsp.	brown sugar	15 mL
2 cups	all-purpose flour	500 mL
1 tbsp.	dried basil	15 mL
1 tsp.	baking powder	5 mL
1 tsp.	baking soda	5 mL
½ tsp.	salt	2 mL
½ cup	tomato juice	125 mL

1. Beat together applesauce, egg substitute, tomato paste and sugar.
2. In a separate bowl, combine flour, basil, baking powder, baking soda and salt.
3. Add flour mixture alternately with tomato juice to the applesauce mixture.
4. Spoon into a 9- x 5-inch (2 L) loaf pan sprayed with cooking spray. Bake for 1 hour or until tester comes out clean.
5. Cool for 5 minutes. Turn out of pan and cool on a rack.

Veal with Lemon-Caper Sauce

SERVES 6

~~~~~~~~~~~~~~~~~~~~~~~~~~~~~~~~~

3 lb.	veal cutlet	1.5 kg
½ tsp.	salt	2 mL
½ tsp.	pepper	2 mL
2 tbsp.	olive oil	30 mL
½ cup	dry vermouth	125 mL
4 tbsp.	fresh lemon juice	60 mL
3 tbsp.	capers	45 mL
½ cup	chopped fresh parsley	125 mL

1. Cut veal into 6 servings and pound into pieces ½ inch (1 cm) thick.
2. Sprinkle half the salt and pepper evenly over meat.
3. Heat oil in a large nonstick skillet over medium heat.
4. Add veal and cook for 2 minutes on each side or until meat is just pink inside.
5. Remove meat from pan; cover to keep warm.
6. Add remaining salt and pepper, vermouth, lemon juice and capers to skillet, scraping pan to loosen browned bits. Cook about 2 minutes until reduced to approximately ⅓ cup (75 mL).
7. Stir in parsley and spoon sauce over veal. Serve immediately.

Garlic Green Beans

SERVES 6

2 tbsp.	olive oil	30 mL
3	cloves garlic, minced	3
1½ lb.	green beans	750 g
½ cup	fresh bread crumbs	125 mL
1	small red pepper, diced	1
	Chopped fresh parsley	

1. Heat oil in a large nonstick skillet or wok. Add garlic and cook until translucent.
2. Add beans and toss in garlic oil mixture. When beans start to turn dark green, add bread crumbs and continue tossing until beans are tender. Turn mixture onto a warmed platter and cover.
3. Sauté red pepper for 1 minute.
4. Garnish beans with red pepper and parsley. Serve immediately.

Preparation Note

You can substitute whole frozen green beans for fresh. Thaw them first.

Mushroom Couscous

SERVES 6

~~~~~~~~~~~~~~~~~~~~~~~~~~~~

Oven: 350°F/180°C

1 tbsp.	vegetable oil	15 mL
4 cups	chopped mushrooms	1 L
1 cup	chopped onions	250 mL
1 cup	chopped celery	250 mL
1 cup	chopped apple	250 mL
3	cloves garlic, minced	3
½ tsp.	dried oregano	2 mL
½ tsp.	dried basil	2 mL
	Salt and pepper to taste	
1 cup	couscous	250 mL
2½ cups	chicken or vegetable broth	625 mL

1. Heat oil in skillet over medium heat. Add mushrooms, onions, celery, apple and garlic. Sauté for 5 minutes.
2. Remove mushroom mixture from heat and stir in oregano, basil, salt, pepper and couscous. Pour into a greased 3-quart (3 L) casserole dish.
3. Add broth and stir well.
4. Cover and bake for 35 minutes.
5. Fluff couscous with fork before serving.

Apple-Cranberry Bread Pudding

SERVES 6

Oven: 350°F/180°C

2 cups	skim milk	500 mL
1	egg	1
2	egg whites	2
½ cup	brown sugar	125 mL
¼ cup	melted butter	50 mL
1 tsp.	vanilla	5 mL
½ cup	dried cranberries	125 mL
1 tsp.	grated lemon zest	5 mL
1 tsp.	cinnamon	5 mL
4 cups	cubed stale egg bread or French bread	1 L
2	apples, peeled and diced	2

1. In a large bowl, whisk together milk, egg, egg whites, sugar, butter and vanilla.
2. Stir in cranberries, lemon zest and cinnamon.
3. Add bread, pushing it under the liquid. Let mixture stand for 10 minutes or until bread is well moistened.
4. Stir in apple.
5. Spray a 6-cup (1.5 L) baking dish with cooking spray. Pour mixture into dish; bake for 50 to 60 minutes or until puffed and set in the centre.

Serving Suggestion

Very nice served with lemon sherbet.

Rakers' Reward

FOR 8

Cheesy Potato-Spinach Soup

(Whole-Wheat Rolls)

Tuscan Tomato Bread Salad

Harvest Apple Torte

Cheesy Potato-Spinach Soup

SERVES 8

2 tbsp.	olive oil	30 mL
3 cups	thinly sliced leeks	750 mL
3 cups	frozen hash brown potatoes, thawed	750 mL
3 cups	chicken broth	750 mL
1½ cups	water	375 mL
	Salt and pepper to taste	
1 package (10 oz.)	frozen spinach	1 package (300 g)
1½ cups	shredded light cheddar cheese	375 mL
1½ cups	skim milk	375 mL

1. Heat olive oil in large saucepan over medium heat. Add leeks and sauté until soft.
2. Add hash browns, broth, water, salt, pepper and spinach. Bring to a boil. Reduce heat and simmer, stirring occasionally.
3. Purée mixture in batches and return to the saucepan.
4. Stir in cheese and milk. Cook until thoroughly heated and cheese is melted.

Preparation Note

Can be made with regular cheddar and the milk of your choice.

Tuscan Tomato Bread Salad

~~~~~~~~~~~~~~~~~~~~~

½	loaf stale crusty Italian bread	½
4	large ripe tomatoes, diced	4
1	red onion, thinly sliced	1
2	cloves garlic, minced	2
¼ cup	chopped fresh basil	50 mL
4 tbsp.	red wine vinegar	60 mL
2 tbsp.	olive oil	30 mL
	Salt and pepper to taste	

1. Cut bread into ½-inch (1 cm) cubes. Set aside.
2. Combine tomatoes, onion, garlic and basil in a large salad bowl.
3. In a jar, combine vinegar, olive oil, salt and pepper. Shake and pour over tomatoes. Chill until ready to add bread.
4. Add bread cubes to the tomato mixture only when ready to serve; toss to combine well. Serve immediately.

Harvest Apple Torte

~~~~~~~~~~~~~~~~~~~~~~~~~~~~~~~~

Oven: 400°F/200°C

6 cups	diced peeled apples	1.5 L
1	egg	1
1	egg white	1
1 tsp.	vanilla	5 mL
1 tbsp.	melted butter	15 mL
1¼ cups	sugar	300 mL
¾ cup	all-purpose flour	175 mL
2 tsp.	baking powder	10 mL
½ cup	raisins	125 mL
½ cup	chopped hazelnuts	125 mL

1. Put apples in a large bowl.
2. In a small bowl, beat egg and egg white, vanilla and melted butter. Pour over apples and mix.
3. Combine sugar, flour and baking powder. Stir into apple mixture.
4. Add raisins and hazelnuts. Stir until well combined.
5. Pour into a greased deep 10-inch (25 cm) pie plate or quiche pan. Bake for 40 minutes or until top is golden.
6. Cut into wedges to serve.

(continued)

Preparation Note

The hazelnuts can be omitted, but they do give a wonderful flavour to this recipe.

Serving Suggestion

Serve with vanilla yogurt or low-fat ice cream.

Four for Fall

FOR 4

*Pork with Potatoes, Apples and
Sour Cream Cider Sauce*

Parsleyed Beets

Marinated Cabbage Salad

Plum Polly

Pork with Potatoes, Apples and Sour Cream Cider Sauce

~~~~~~~~~~~~~~~~~~~~~~

Oven: 400°F/200°C

1½ lb.	pork tenderloin	750 g
1 tsp.	dried sage	5 mL
2 tbsp.	olive oil	30 mL
1	large onion, cut into wedges	1
1 lb.	small red potatoes, cut in half	500 g
3	apples, cut into 1-inch (2.5 cm) cubes	3
1½ cups	apple cider	375 mL
1 cup	chicken broth	250 mL
½ cup	calvados (apple brandy)	125 mL
	Salt and pepper to taste	
½ cup	no-fat or low-fat sour cream	125 mL

1. Trim tenderloin and sprinkle with sage. Brown in half the olive oil in a heavy skillet. Remove meat from pan and set aside.
2. Add the rest of the oil to skillet. Add onion and sauté for 5 minutes.
3. Put pork, onions and potatoes in a small roasting pan. Bake, uncovered, for 15 minutes.
4. Add apples and bake an additional 20 minutes or until potatoes are tender.
5. Remove pork and potato mixture from pan. Keep warm.

6. Add cider, broth, calvados, salt and pepper to pan, scraping pan to loosen browned bits. Boil over high heat for about 8 minutes.
7. Remove sauce from heat; stir in sour cream, stirring with a whisk to blend well.
8. Return to low heat and simmer for 1 minute.
9. Cut pork into ¼-inch (5 mm) slices. Arrange pork on plates. Top with potato mixture and a scoop of sour cream gravy.

Preparation Note

For the alcohol-free version, increase the apple cider to 2 cups (500 mL). You can also use white wine or brandy instead of calvados.

Parsleyed Beets

SERVES 4

1 tsp.	olive oil	5 mL
2 tbsp.	vegetable broth	30 mL
3	cloves garlic, finely chopped	3
½ cup	chopped fresh parsley	125 mL
¼ tsp.	salt	1 mL
3 cups	sliced cooked beets	750 mL
1 tbsp.	fresh lemon juice	15 mL

1. Heat oil and broth in a heavy saucepan and sauté garlic.
2. Add parsley and sprinkle with salt. Cover and cook over low heat until parsley wilts.
3. Add beets and lemon juice; toss. Cover until heated through.

Marinated Cabbage Salad

¾ cup	vinegar	175 mL
¼ cup	water	50 mL
⅔ cup	sugar	150 mL
1 tsp.	celery seed	5 mL
1 tsp.	mustard seed	5 mL
½ tsp.	turmeric	2 mL
½ tsp.	salt	2 mL
½	small head cabbage, shredded	½
1	carrot, grated	1
1	small onion, minced	1
½	green pepper, finely chopped	½

1. Put vinegar, water, sugar, celery seed, mustard seed, turmeric and salt in a small saucepan; bring to a boil. Let cool.
2. In a large bowl, toss cabbage, carrot, onion and green pepper.
3. Pour cooled dressing over cabbage. Store in a tightly sealed container in the fridge. Let stand several hours before serving.

Preparation Note

Can be stored for a week in the fridge.

Plum Polly

~~~~~~~~~~~~~~~~~~~~

Oven: 400°F/200°C

5 cups	quartered ripe plums	1.25 L
½ cup	brown sugar	125 mL
½ cup	oats	125 mL
½ cup	chopped hazelnuts	125 mL
3 tbsp.	all-purpose flour	45 mL
3 tbsp.	light butter, cut in pieces	45 mL

1. Place plums in a greased baking dish.
2. Mix the remaining ingredients together; sprinkle over plums.
3. Bake for 40 minutes or until golden.

Georgian Bay Bounty

FOR 4

Date with a Salad

The Watchers' White Fish

Two-Colour Oven Fries

Seasoned Carrots

Pineapple-Carrot Cake

Date with a Salad

~~~~~~~~~~~~~~~~~~~~~~~~~~~~

2	tart eating apples, peeled and diced	2
2 tsp.	lemon juice	10 mL
1	small turnip, peeled and finely grated	1
10	pitted dates, coarsely chopped	10
1¼ tsp.	sugar	6 mL
¼ cup	no-fat yogurt	50 mL
	Mixed salad greens	

1. Toss diced apples with lemon juice.
2. Add turnip, dates and sugar. Mix thoroughly.
3. Stir in yogurt. Chill.
4. Serve on a bed of mixed greens.

The Watchers' White Fish

SERVES 4

_____

Oven: 375°F/190°C

1½ lb.	whitefish fillets (sole, pickerel or perch)	750 g
1	onion, sliced	1
¾ cup	no-fat sour cream	175 mL
1 tsp.	paprika	5 mL
½ cup	shredded light Swiss cheese	125 mL

1. Place fish fillets in a greased baking dish.
2. Cover fillets with slices of onion.
3. Combine sour cream and paprika. Pour over fish.
4. Top with cheese.
5. Bake for 20 minutes or until fish flakes easily.

Preparation Note

Can be cooked in the microwave. Cover dish with plastic wrap. Cook on High for 6 minutes.

Two-Colour Oven Fries

~~~~~~~~~~~~~~~~~~~~~~~

Oven: 400°F/200°C

4	white potatoes, peeled	4
4	sweet potatoes, peeled	4
2 tbsp.	olive oil	30 mL
	Salt and pepper to taste	

1. Cut potatoes into thin strips.
2. Place olive oil, salt and pepper in a large bowl.
3. Toss potatoes in the oil mixture. Arrange in single layers on baking sheets.
4. Bake for 35 minutes, turning during cooking, or until potatoes are tender.

Seasoned Carrots

~~~~~~~~~~~~~~~~~~~~~~

10	carrots, peeled and julienned	10
1 tsp.	olive oil	5 mL
1 tbsp.	vegetable broth	15 mL
1	medium onion, halved and sliced	1
2	cloves garlic, minced	2
1 tbsp.	chopped fresh parsley	15 mL
	Pepper to taste	

1. Steam carrots until just tender.
2. Heat oil and broth in a large skillet; sauté onion and garlic until translucent.
3. Add carrots, parsley and pepper. Cook, covered, over medium heat for 5 minutes.

Pineapple-Carrot Cake

YIELDS 1 BUNDT CAKE

Oven: 350°F/180°C

3 tbsp.	applesauce	45 mL
2 tbsp.	canola oil	30 mL
5	egg whites	5
1 cup	sugar	250 mL
1 cup	shredded carrots	250 mL
1 can (14 oz.)	crushed pineapple	1 can (398 g)
1 tsp.	vanilla	5 mL
2 cups	all-purpose flour	500 mL
2 tsp.	baking powder	10 mL
1 tsp.	baking soda	5 mL
1 tsp.	cinnamon	5 mL
½ tsp.	nutmeg	2 mL

Pineapple Topping

3	egg whites	3
1 tsp.	vanilla	5 mL
1 tsp.	sugar	5 mL
4 tbsp.	crushed pineapple	60 mL

1. In a large bowl, combine the applesauce, oil and egg whites. Mix with an electric beater until frothy.

2. Add sugar, carrots, 1 cup (250 mL) crushed pineapple with the juice and vanilla. Mix well.
3. Combine flour, baking powder, baking soda, cinnamon and nutmeg; add to the carrot mixture. Stir until well blended.
4. Spray an 8-cup (2 L) bundt pan with cooking spray and dust with flour. Pour batter into pan. Bake for 40 minutes or until tester comes out clean.
5. For the topping, beat egg whites until stiff.
6. Add vanilla and sugar; beat until well combined.
7. Drain 4 tbsp. (60 mL) crushed pineapple. Fold into topping. Spoon over cake and serve immediately.

Masquerade Dinner

FOR 4

Pumpkin Soup

My Very Best Salmon

Scalloped Turnip

Snow Pea Stir-Fry

Apple Cream

Pumpkin Soup

1	medium onion, chopped	1
1 tbsp.	canola oil	15 mL
3 cups	chicken broth	750 mL
2 cups	canned pure pumpkin	500 mL
2 cups	skim milk	500 mL
½ tsp.	ginger	2 mL
½ tsp.	nutmeg	2 mL
½ tsp.	allspice	2 mL
3 tbsp.	port (or to taste)	45 mL

1. In a soup kettle, sauté onion in oil until transparent.
2. Add chicken broth, pumpkin and skim milk. Heat thoroughly but do not boil.
3. Stir in spices.
4. Remove from heat and stir in port (if desired).

Serving Suggestion

Add more milk if too thick.

My Very Best Salmon

~~~~~~

4	salmon fillets	4
⅓ cup	rye whisky	75 mL
¼ cup	vegetable broth	50 mL
4 tbsp.	light soy sauce	60 mL
2 tbsp.	brown sugar	30 mL
2 tbsp.	white wine vinegar	30 mL
1 tbsp.	garlic powder	15 mL
½ tsp.	pepper	2 mL

1. Place fillets in a shallow pan. Mix together all the other ingredients; pour over the salmon. Marinate for at least 2 hours, turning occasionally.
2. Barbecue salmon 4 inches (10 cm) above coals for 7 minutes or until cooked through. Turn and grill for 1 minute more. Serve immediately.

Scalloped Turnip

~~~~~~~~~~~~~~~~~~~~~~~~~~~~~~~

Oven: 350°F/180°C

4 cups	thinly sliced turnip	1 L
1	large onion, sliced in rings	1
2 tbsp.	all-purpose flour	30 mL
3 tbsp.	light butter	45 mL
1½ cups	skim milk	375 mL

1. Spray a 10-inch (25 cm) baking dish. Arrange in it a layer of turnip and onion rings.
2. Sprinkle with some of the flour and dot with butter. Repeat layers.
3. Heat milk and pour over turnip.
4. Cover baking dish; bake for 30 minutes. Uncover and bake 1 hour more.

Snow Pea Stir-Fry

~~~~~~~~~~~~~~~~~~~~~~~~~

1 tbsp.	olive oil	15 mL
1 tbsp.	sesame oil	15 mL
1 tbsp.	sesame seeds	15 mL
½ tsp.	ginger	2 mL
1	medium red pepper, cubed	1
½ lb.	snow peas	250 g
1 can (8 oz.)	water chestnuts, sliced	1 can (227 mL)

1. Place oils, sesame seeds and ginger in a wok or frying pan. Heat over medium-high heat until sesame seeds are golden.
2. Add red pepper, snow peas and water chestnuts. Stir-fry until vegetables are tender. Serve immediately.

Apple Cream

~~~~~~~~~~~~~~~~~~~~~~~~~~~~~~~~

1 cup	plain no-fat yogurt	250 mL
3 tbsp.	maple syrup	45 mL
⅓ cup	fresh orange juice	75 mL
2 tbsp.	fresh lemon juice	30 mL
2 tbsp.	sugar (or to taste)	30 mL
6	apples, peeled	6

1. Mix yogurt and maple syrup together. Chill until ready to serve.
2. Mix orange juice, lemon juice and sugar in a large bowl.
3. Grate peeled apples into the juices. Mix well because the juice helps to prevent the apples from discolouring. Chill.
4. When ready to serve, combine the yogurt mixture with the apples.

6

Winter

~~~~~~~~~~

Winterlude

Brunch amongst the Wrappings

A Christmas Celebration

Boxing Day Blowout

A Fresh Start

A Winter's Eve

Mom's Comfort Food

Après Ski

Tandoori Treasure

*T*HERE ARE TIMES when we have said that a Georgian Bay winter is just as beautiful as a Georgian Bay summer. Many doubt our word, but it's true! Because here, in the snow belt, we have "real" winter—lots of snow and many days of cold, very very cold, bright days. When a thick layer of ice fills the Bay, it becomes the winter playground for skiers, skaters and snowmobilers. At night when you look across Nottawasaga Bay to Collingwood, you can see the ski hills ablaze with lights for the benefit of the downhill skiers who are not quite ready to call it a day. There are endless trails for snowshoeing and cross-country skiing near Lafontaine and Awenda Park, and in Midland and Penetang Bays, small villages of ice huts provide shelter for the "true" fishermen.

As Christmas approaches the parties begin. A favourite of ours is the annual Georgian Bay Gourmet Christmas Party, which has been a popular event for more than twenty years. Sounds like a rather fancy gathering, but there have only ever been four invited guests . . . four good friends—just the four of us! We spend the evening with some very good wine and our favourite treat: a big bag of shrimp. We chat about the past year and what is to come (perhaps another cookbook?!) and above all, we laugh. We exchange gifts: something home-made, something unique, something from the heart. We pull out the photo album that chronicles this long friendship and we laugh at our dresses and hairdos. We never go home without posing for the annual group photograph. For us, this will always be a very special Christmas party.

And then, finally, the holidays are here and once again our children come home. They can hardly wait for Mom's Comfort Food and Brunch amongst the Wrappings, and no matter how old they are, the traditional Christmas dinner has always been the big favourite. But why not break with tradition and try our light and delicious Merry Chocolate Cheesecake to finish off the feast? The kids won't miss the Christmas pudding!

Throughout our glorious winter, friends enjoy midnight cross-country skiing along torch-lit trails. Some of us attend New Year's Eve bonfires down at the snow-covered beach, dressed in tuxedos and evening gowns along with our snowmobile boots. And right at the stroke of midnight, the sky above the frozen Bay is filled with a myriad of multicoloured fireworks.

Offer your guests our Winter's Eve menu as you welcome in the New Year. But if your preference is to stay by the fire on a cold winter's night, enjoy Winterlude with very good friends.

The Penetanguishene Winter Carnival has been around a lot longer than we have! And even though our kids are all grown up now, on the third weekend in February you can't miss the parade down Main Street, or the ice sculptures at the bottom of the hill near Penetang Town Dock. After a heart-warming bowl of pea soup, it's over to Church Street for the toboggan races, and later in the evening you can always enjoy a dance or two at the Legion or the arena.

And then before you know it, it's March . . .

Winterlude

FOR 6

Carrot-Orange Soup

Pear and Blue Cheese Salad

Chicken Prosciutto Packages

Grapes 'n' Rice

Grilled Tomatoes

New Age Grapes Juanita

Carrot-Orange Soup

6 to 8	carrots, sliced	6 to 8
2	medium onions, chopped	2
2 tbsp.	margarine	30 mL
4 cups	chicken stock	1 L
2 cups	orange juice	500 mL
1 cup	skim milk	250 mL
	Salt and pepper to taste	
	Sprigs of fresh dill	

1. In a large pot, sauté carrots and onions in margarine until onions are tender.
2. Add chicken stock and bring to a boil. Reduce heat and simmer for 15 minutes. Remove from heat. Allow mixture to cool slightly.
3. Purée mixture. Return to pot and stir in orange juice. Gently reheat mixture, without boiling. Stir in skim milk and heat through.
4. Garnish each serving with a sprig of fresh dill.

Serving Suggestion

This soup is delicious served hot or cold.

Pear and Blue Cheese Salad

SERVES 6

8 cups	mixed salad greens	2 L
3	ripe pears, cored and thinly sliced	3
1 tbsp.	honey mustard	15 mL
1 tbsp.	balsamic vinegar	15 mL
3 tbsp.	olive oil	45 mL
	Salt and pepper	
½ cup	walnut pieces	125 mL
4 oz.	blue cheese, crumbled	125 g

1. Place greens and sliced pears in a bowl.
2. In a small bowl, combine mustard and vinegar; slowly whisk in the oil. Season with salt and pepper.
3. Pour dressing over the salad and toss.
4. Serve on individual plates, garnished with walnuts and blue cheese.

Chicken Prosciutto Packages

~~~~~~~~~~~~~~~~~~~~~~~~~~~~~~~~~~~~~~

Oven: 350°F/180°C

3 tbsp.	green peppercorn mustard	45 mL
1 tbsp.	chopped fresh thyme	15 mL
2 tsp.	liquid honey	10 mL
	Pepper	
6	boneless, skinless chicken breasts	6
12	fresh sage leaves	12
12	slices prosciutto	12
2 tbsp.	olive oil	30 mL

1. In a small bowl, stir together mustard, thyme, honey and pepper.
2. Brush mixture evenly over each chicken breasts; place 2 sage leaves lengthwise over each breast.
3. Wrap 2 slices of prosciutto crosswise around each breast, tucking ends underneath.
4. Place chicken on a foil-lined baking sheet. Brush each breast with olive oil.
5. Bake for 30 minutes or until chicken is no longer pink inside.

Preparation Note

After step 3, chicken can be covered and refrigerated for up to 6 hours.

Grapes 'n' Rice

SERVES 6 TO 8

1¼ cups	wild rice	300 mL
1 tbsp.	olive oil	15 mL
1½ cups	diced celery	375 mL
1 cup	chopped onions	250 mL
2 tbsp.	chopped fresh thyme	30 mL
2 cups	halved red grapes	500 mL
1½ cups	slivered almonds	375 mL
¾ cup	sherry	175 mL
	Salt and pepper to taste	

1. Cook rice according to package directions. Drain if necessary and set aside in a medium bowl.
2. Heat oil in a large frying pan. Sauté celery and onions for 3 minutes.
3. Reduce heat and stir in thyme, red grapes and almonds. Cook until heated through.
4. Combine this mixture with the cooked rice.
5. Add sherry and season with salt and pepper.

Preparation Note

Rice may be prepared ahead of time and reheated.

Grilled Tomatoes

SERVES 6 TO 8

Oven: 350°F/180°C

1 tbsp.	melted margarine	15 mL
1	clove garlic, minced	1
½ cup	dried bread crumbs	125 mL
1 tsp.	dried oregano	5 mL
4	large tomatoes, cut in half crosswise	4
	Dried thyme to taste	

1. Combine melted margarine, garlic, bread crumbs and oregano.
2. Arrange tomatoes cut side up on a baking sheet. Sprinkle tomatoes with thyme; place a layer of the crumb mixture on each tomato.
3. Bake for 20 minutes or until heated through.
4. Serve hot.

New Age Grapes Juanita

SERVES 6

2 lb.	seedless green grapes	1 kg.
½ cup	plain no-fat yogurt	125 mL
3 tbsp.	maple syrup (or to taste)	45 mL

1. Remove stems from grapes and place in a fruit bowl.
2. Combine yogurt and maple syrup; pour over grapes. Stir well until grapes are well coated. Chill.
3. Serve in stemmed glasses.

Brunch amongst the Wrappings

FOR 8

Baked French Toast

Coriander Blueberries

Cinnamon-Almond Biscotti

Café Blanc

Baked French Toast

~~~~~~~~~~~~~~~~~~~~~~~~~~~~~~~~~~

Oven: 350°F/180°C

1 cup	maple syrup	250 mL
1	loaf French bread	1
4	eggs	4
4	egg whites	4
1½ cups	skim milk	375 mL
2 tsp.	vanilla	10 mL
1 tsp.	nutmeg	5 mL

1. Lightly spray 9- x 13-inch (3/3.5 L) baking dish with vegetable spray.
2. Pour in maple syrup.
3. Slice French bread into eight 2-inch (5 cm) slices and place in one layer over syrup.
4. In a bowl, beat together eggs, egg whites, milk, vanilla and nutmeg.
5. Pour egg mixture over bread. Cover and refrigerate overnight.
6. Bake for 40 to 45 minutes or until golden brown.

Coriander Blueberries

3 cups	blueberries	750 mL
1 cup	no-fat sour cream	250 mL
2 tbsp.	brown sugar	30 mL
1 tsp.	ground coriander	5 mL

1. Place blueberries in individual serving dishes.
2. In a bowl, combine sour cream, sugar and coriander. Put a dollop on top of each serving.

Cinnamon-Almond Biscotti

Oven: 350°F/180°C

2	eggs	2
2	egg whites	2
1 tsp.	vanilla	5 mL
1 cup	sugar	250 mL
1 cup	finely ground almonds	250 mL
2 tsp.	cinnamon	10 mL
3 cups	all-purpose flour	750 mL
1 tsp.	baking soda	5 mL
4 oz.	semisweet chocolate (optional)	125 g

1. Spray cookie sheet with cooking spray.
2. In a large bowl, beat together eggs, egg whites and vanilla.
3. Add sugar, almonds and cinnamon; beat again.
4. Add flour and baking soda; beat slowly until a dough forms.
5. Turn dough out onto a floured surface. With your hands, form dough into 2 balls. Roll each ball into a log, using more flour if too sticky. Form 2 logs approximately 2 inches (5 cm) wide by 8 inches (20 cm) long. Place on cookie sheet about 3 inches (8 cm) apart.
6. Bake for 40 minutes; remove from oven and reduce heat to 275°F (140°C).

(continued)

7. On cutting board, cut the logs diagonally into ½-inch (1 cm) slices. Place biscuits cut side up on cookie sheet; return to oven to bake another 20 minutes.
8. Turn the heat off and leave biscotti to crisp in oven for 15 minutes. Cool completely on wire rack.
9. Melt chocolate squares (if desired) in the top of a double boiler, stirring once or twice. Dip one end of each biscotti into the chocolate and cool.

Preparation Note

Store in an airtight container or freeze until ready to use.

Café Blanc

~~~~~~~~~~~~~~~~~~~~~~

4 cups	freshly brewed coffee	1 L
4 cups	1% scalded milk	1 L
	Sweetener to taste	
8	cinnamon sticks	8

1. Pour equal parts of hot coffee and hot milk into coffee mugs.
2. Sweeten to taste. Add a cinnamon stick to each mug as a stirrer.

A Christmas Celebration

FOR 8

Roast Stuffed Turkey

Creamy Mashed Potatoes

Cranberry Cream Salad

Holiday Brussels Sprouts

Pared Red Coleslaw

(Carrots)

Merry Chocolate Cheesecake

Roast Stuffed Turkey

~~~~~~

Oven: 450°F/230°C

10–12 lb.	turkey	5–6 kg
	Turkey Stuffing (below)	

1. Wash turkey inside and out. Pat dry.
2. Place stuffing in cavity. Close cavity with skewers and string. Draw the thighs close to the body and tie firmly with string. Hold the wings in place with a long skewer or tie with string.
3. Place turkey on a rack in a roasting pan, legs up.
4. Put the turkey in the preheated oven and reduce to 350°F (180°C). Allow 20 minutes per pound (500 g) cooking time, and baste frequently.

Turkey Stuffing

Yields 5 cups/1.25 L

1 lb.	dried bread, diced or torn	500 g
1 cup	finely chopped onion	250 mL
1 cup	finely chopped celery	250 mL
2 tsp.	dried sage	10 mL
1 tsp.	dried rosemary	5 mL
¾ cup	vegetable broth	175 mL

(continued)

1. Mix bread and seasonings together in a large bowl and drizzle with broth; toss. If the bread is very dry, add a little more broth.

Serving Suggestion

To reduce fat, remove skin when carving and forget the gravy.

Creamy Mashed Potatoes

2	cloves garlic	2
12	medium potatoes	12
1 cup	no-fat sour cream	250 mL
	Salt and pepper to taste	

1. Boil potatoes and garlic cloves until potatoes are tender. Discard garlic. Mash potatoes.
2. Add sour cream, salt and pepper; whip well.

Cranberry Cream Salad

1 package (3 oz.)	cherry gelatine	1 package (85 g)
1 cup	hot water	250 mL
1 can (12 oz.)	cranberry sauce	1 can (375 g)
½ cup	chopped walnuts	125 mL
1 cup	finely diced celery	250 mL
1½ cups	no-fat sour cream	375 mL

1. Dissolve cherry gelatine in hot water. Chill until partially set.
2. Add cranberry sauce, walnuts and celery. Stir until well combined.
3. Fold in sour cream and pour into a 6-cup (1.5 L) mould. Chill until firm.

Preparation Note

If using cooked fresh cranberries, use orange juice instead of water to give a different flavour.

Holiday Brussels Sprouts

SERVES 8

2 lb.	Brussels sprouts	1 kg
2 tbsp.	butter	30 mL
¼ cup	fine dry bread crumbs	50 mL
2 tbsp.	chopped fresh parsley	30 mL

1. Boil or steam Brussels sprouts until tender and drain.
2. Melt butter in a small pan. Stir in bread crumbs and parsley.
3. Spoon mixture over sprouts and toss lightly.

Pared Red Coleslaw

~~~~~~~~~~~~~~~~~~~~~~~~~~~~~~~~~~

3 cups	shredded red cabbage	750 mL
1	green pepper, chopped	1
1	small onion, sliced	1
2	stalks celery, chopped	2
1	pear, diced	1
	Rice Vinegar Mayo (below)	
	Salt and freshly ground pepper	
	to taste	

1. In a large bowl, combine vegetables and pear.
2. Add dressing and season with salt and pepper.

Rice Vinegar Mayo

½ cup	no-fat mayonnaise	125 mL
2 tbsp.	rice vinegar	30 mL

1. Put mayonnaise and vinegar in a jar and shake well.

Merry Chocolate Cheesecake

Oven: 350°F/180°C

2 cups	low-fat graham cracker crumbs	500 mL
¼ cup	melted light butter	50 mL
¼ tsp.	cinnamon	1 mL
1½ lb.	light cream cheese	750 g
1 cup	sugar	250 mL
2	eggs	2
2	egg whites	2
½ cup	cocoa	125 mL
¼–⅓ cup	hot water	50–75 mL
1 tsp.	vanilla	5 mL
2 cups	no-fat sour cream	500 mL
	Icing sugar	

1. Mix graham cracker crumbs with butter and cinnamon. Press into the bottom of a 9-inch (2.5 L) springform pan. Chill.
2. In a large bowl or food processor, beat cream cheese until light and fluffy.
3. Beat in sugar. Beat in eggs 1 at a time. Beat in egg whites.
4. In a small bowl, mix cocoa powder and hot water to dissolve cocoa. Add a little more water if needed.
5. Beat dissolved cocoa into the cheese mixture along with the vanilla.
6. Add sour cream and mix well. Pour over crumb base.

(continued)

7. Bake approximately 1 hour and 10 minutes. The cake may be a bit soft but will firm as it chills. Cool at room temperature and then chill for 6 hours or overnight. Cake sometimes cracks on top.
8. Dust with sifted icing sugar just before serving.

Preparation Note

Cocoa powder is fat-free, so you get the chocolate flavour without all of the fat in chocolate.

Serving Suggestion

Drizzle some puréed raspberries over each slice.

Our original recipe in *Georgian Bay Gourmet Winter Entertaining* was a big hit. This lighter version is great and can also be frozen!

Boxing Day Blowout

FOR 6

Turkey Paella

Crunchy Pea Salad

Irish Soda Bread

(Clementines)

Turkey Paella

~~~~~~~~~~~~~~~~~~~~~~

Oven: 350°F/180°C

1 can (14 oz.)	tomatoes	1 can (398 mL)
2½ cups	tomato juice	625 mL
¼ cup	chopped onion	50 mL
¼ cup	chopped green pepper	50 mL
1 tsp.	salt	5 mL
2	cloves garlic, minced	2
1 cup	rice	250 mL
3 cups	diced cooked turkey	750 mL
1 cup	button mushrooms	250 mL
¼ cup	sliced olives	50 mL
1 can (10 oz.)	baby clams, drained	1 can (284 mL)
	Grated low-fat Parmesan cheese (optional)	

1. In a large saucepan, combine tomatoes, tomato juice, onion, green pepper, salt and garlic.
2. Stir in rice. Cover and bring to a boil.
3. Remove from heat and stir in turkey, mushrooms, olives and clams. Turn into a 3-quart (3 L) casserole dish.
4. Bake, uncovered, for 45 minutes or until rice is tender, stirring occasionally.
5. Sprinkle with grated Parmesan before serving if desired.

Crunchy Pea Salad

~~~~~~~~~~~~~~~

3 cups	frozen green peas, thawed	750 mL
⅓ cup	chopped red onion	75 mL
⅓ cup	chopped celery	75 mL
¼ cup	no-fat mayonnaise	50 mL
⅓ cup	shredded low-fat cheddar cheese	75 mL
¼ cup	roasted peanuts	50 mL

1. In a large bowl, combine all ingredients and mix well. Serve chilled or at room temperature.

Irish Soda Bread

Oven: 350°F/180°C

2 cups	all-purpose flour	500 mL
1½ cups	whole-wheat flour	375 mL
½ cup	bran	125 mL
⅓ cup	sugar	75 mL
1½ tsp.	baking soda	7 mL
1½ tsp.	salt	7 mL
1½–2 cups	buttermilk	375–500 mL

1. Place all dry ingredients in a large bowl and stir together.
2. Add buttermilk; stir until mixture is thick and sticky. Form a ball.
3. On a floured board, divide into 2 small rounds or shape into 1 large round. Score top with an X before baking.
4. Place on baking sheet and bake 45 minutes or until knife inserted comes out clean.

A Fresh Start

FOR 8

(Champagne and Orange Juice)

Mediterranean Strata

(Fresh Rolls)

Tangy Fruit Salad

Good Morning Orange Muffins

Mediterranean Strata

SERVES 8

Oven: 350°F/180°C

2 tbsp.	olive oil	30 mL
2	large onions, sliced	2
2 tsp.	minced garlic	10 mL
½ cup	chopped roasted red peppers	125 mL
½ cup	chopped pitted green olives	125 mL
½ cup	chopped oil-packed sun-dried tomatoes	125 mL
½ cup	chopped artichoke hearts	125 mL
3 cups	cubed Italian bread	750 mL
1 cup	crumbled low-fat feta cheese	250 mL
2	eggs	2
5	egg whites	5
1 cup	low-fat chicken broth	250 mL
¼ cup	dry white wine	50 mL
	Salt and pepper to taste	

1. In a large skillet, heat olive oil over medium heat. Sauté onions and garlic until onions are golden. Remove from heat.
2. Stir in peppers, olives, sun-dried tomatoes and artichokes.
3. Spray a 10-inch (25 cm) quiche pan with cooking spray.
4. Place bread cubes in quiche pan and top with onion mixture and crumbled feta.

5. In a large bowl, beat together eggs, egg whites, broth, wine, salt and pepper. Pour over bread mixture.
6. Bake for 35 to 40 minutes or until set.
7. Let stand 10 minutes before serving.

Preparation Note

Can be assembled, covered and refrigerated overnight.

Tangy Fruit Salad

~~~~~~~~~~~~~~~~~~~~~

4 cups	sliced bananas	1 L
4 cups	cubed cantaloupe	1 L
1	avocado, sliced	1
	Lettuce leaves	
	Tangy Dressing (below)	

1. Arrange fruit and avocado on 8 lettuce-lined plates.
2. Drizzle Tangy Dressing over top.

Tangy Dressing

Yields ¾ cup/175 mL

2 tbsp.	sugar	30 mL
1 tbsp.	vegetable oil	15 mL
⅓ cup	lemon juice	75 mL
¼ cup	water	50 mL
1 tsp.	celery seed	5 mL
1 tsp.	dry mustard	5 mL
1 tsp.	paprika	5 mL
	Salt and pepper to taste	

1. Place ingredients in a blender or jar. Blend or shake until well mixed.

Good Morning Orange Muffins

YIELDS 1 DOZEN

~~~~~~~~~~~~~~~~~~~~~~~~~~~~~

Oven: 350°F/180°C

1	seedless orange	1
½ cup	orange juice	125 mL
1	egg	1
⅓ cup	applesauce	75 mL
3 tbsp.	canola oil	45 mL
⅔ cup	sugar	150 mL
1½ cups	all-purpose flour	375 mL
1 tsp.	baking soda	5 mL
1 tsp.	baking powder	5 mL
	Pinch salt	
½ cup	raisins	125 mL

1. Cut orange, including skin, into pieces and drop into food processor. Blend until pulp and rind are finely chopped.
2. Add orange juice, egg, applesauce and oil. Blend again.
3. Blend in sugar.
4. Sift together flour, baking soda, baking powder and salt. Add in thirds to the food processor, processing each time just enough to combine thoroughly.
5. Add raisins and stir lightly with a spoon.
6. Spoon batter into greased muffin tins or papers. Bake for 20 minutes or until golden.
7. Store in a plastic container or freeze.

A Winter's Eve

FOR 8

Sherried Tomato Consommé

Rolled Sirloin Roast of Beef

Cabbage and Horseradish Cream

Roasted Dijon Potatoes

Lemon-Dilled Carrots

Minted Peas

Lemon Surprise

Sherried Tomato Consommé

~~~~~~~~~~~~~~~~~~~~~~~~~~~~~~~~~~~~~

6 cups	chicken broth	1.5 L
3 cups	canned plum tomatoes in juice	750 mL
2 tbsp.	sugar	30 mL
	Salt and pepper to taste	
½ cup	medium-dry sherry	125 mL
	Thinly sliced chives or green onions for garnish	

1. In a saucepan, combine broth, tomatoes, sugar, salt and pepper. Bring to a boil over medium-high heat. Reduce heat and simmer 15 minutes.
2. Stir in sherry and heat through. Ladle into heated bowls.
3. Garnish with chives or green onions.

Rolled Sirloin Roast of Beef

SERVES 8

~~~~~~~~~~~~~~~~~~~~~~~~~~~~

Oven: 350°F/180°C

4-lb.	sirloin roast, boned and rolled	2 kg
10	cloves garlic, sliced	10
2 tbsp.	peppercorns	30 mL
1 tsp.	dried oregano	5 mL
½ tsp.	dried thyme	2 mL
1 tbsp.	olive oil	15 mL

1. Trim most of the exterior fat from roast and pat dry.
2. With a sharp knife, make small slits in roast (do not disturb string). Insert garlic slice into each slit.
3. Place peppercorns between sheets of waxed paper and gently crush with mallet. Remove top sheet of paper and mix in oregano and thyme. Spread mixture evenly over paper.
4. Brush roast with oil. Roll roast carefully in peppercorn mixture to coat evenly. Place roast in roasting pan. Roast in preheated oven for 75 minutes or until meat thermometer reads 160°F (70°C) for medium, 140°F (60°C) for rare.
5. Remove from oven, loosely cover with foil and let stand 15 to 30 minutes.
6. Thinly slice meat; serve on warm platter.

Cabbage and Horseradish Cream

~~~~~~~~~~~~~~~~~~~~~~~~~~~

1	small cabbage, shredded	1
1	onion, sliced	1
1 tbsp.	olive oil	15 mL
½ cup	no-fat sour cream	125 mL
2 tbsp.	chopped green onions	30 mL
1 tbsp.	prepared horseradish	15 mL
1 tbsp.	sugar	15 mL

1. Stir-fry cabbage and onion in oil in a nonstick skillet until golden; do not overcook.
2. Combine sour cream, green onions, horseradish and sugar in a small bowl.
3. Place cabbage and sour cream mixtures in a serving bowl and toss until cabbage is evenly coated. Serve.

Serving Suggestion

May be prepared ahead of time and warmed before serving.

Roasted Dijon Potatoes

Oven: 350°F/180°C

½ cup	Dijon mustard	125 mL
1 tbsp.	olive oil	15 mL
3	cloves garlic, chopped	3
1 tsp.	dried basil	10 mL
1 tsp.	dried oregano	10 mL
1 tsp.	dried thyme	10 mL
10	medium red potatoes, cut in chunks (do not peel)	10

1. Put all the ingredients except potatoes in a jar and shake well.
2. Pour mixture over potatoes and toss.
3. Place potatoes in one layer in a sprayed ovenproof dish and bake for 1 hour or until potatoes are tender. Turn potatoes once halfway through cooking.

Lemon-Dilled Carrots

~~~~~~~~~~~~~~~~~~~~~~~~~~~~~~~~~

1 tsp.	olive oil	5 mL
4 cups	diagonally sliced carrots	1 L
¼ cup	fat-free, sodium-reduced chicken broth	50 mL
1 tbsp.	fresh lemon juice	15 mL
1 tsp.	grated lemon zest	5 mL
½ tsp.	celery salt	2 mL
¼ tsp.	black pepper	1 mL
1 tbsp.	chopped fresh dill (or 1 tsp./5 mL dried)	15 mL

1. Heat oil in a large nonstick pan over medium-high heat. Add carrots and sauté 3 minutes.
2. Stir in broth, lemon juice, lemon zest, celery salt and pepper. Cover and reduce heat to medium-low. Cook for 10 minutes or until tender, stirring occasionally.
3. Remove from heat; stir in dill. Serve.

Minted Peas

~~~~~~~~~~~~~~~~~~~~~~~~~~~~~

4 cups	fresh or frozen peas	1 L
	Boiling water	
	Salt	
3	mint leaves	3
1 tsp.	butter	5 mL

1. Drop peas into boiling water (it should just cover peas).
2. Add salt and mint leaves.
3. Boil until tender.
4. Place cooked peas in serving dish; top with butter.

Lemon Surprise

~~~~~~~~~~~~~~~~~~~~~~~~~~~~

1¼ cups	sugar	300 mL
4 tbsp.	cornstarch	60 mL
	Pinch salt	
1½ cups	warm water	375 mL
	Juice of 2 lemons	
	Zest of 1 lemon	
1	egg yolk	1
3	egg whites	3
¼ tsp.	cream of tartar	1 mL
1 tsp.	sugar	5 mL
	Vanilla Custard (page 300)	
	Lime twists or mint sprigs for garnish	

1. In a saucepan, mix together sugar, cornstarch and salt.
2. Place over medium heat, and slowly stir in water, stirring until mixture thickens.
3. Add lemon juice and zest. Boil, stirring, 1 minute.
4. Lightly beat egg yolk in a small bowl. Slowly pour some of the lemon mixture into the yolk, beating continuously. Then blend back into the saucepan. Boil for another minute, stirring constantly.
5. Remove mixture from the heat and cool for about 15 minutes. Place pot in the sink with some cold water to speed up the cooling.
6. Beat egg whites until foamy and add the cream of tartar.
7. Add 1 tsp. (5 mL) sugar and continue to beat until whites are stiff and glossy.

(continued)

8. When the lemon mixture has cooled somewhat, fold the meringue into the lemon mixture until well blended.
9. Pour into dessert bowls and top with warm Vanilla Custard. Garnish with a twist of lime or a sprig of mint.

Serving Suggestion

The lemon pudding can be served without the Vanilla Custard, although the recipe then serves fewer people.

Vanilla Custard

⅓ cup	sugar	75 mL
¼ cup	all-purpose flour	50 mL
	Pinch salt	
1¼ cups	skim milk	300 mL
1	egg	1
1½ tsp.	vanilla	7 mL

1. Combine sugar, flour and salt in a medium saucepan.
2. Stir in milk and cook, stirring, over medium heat until mixture is thickened and bubbly. Cook 2 more minutes.
3. Beat egg in a small bowl. Stir some of the hot mixture into the egg. Stir well and then pour back into the saucepan. Cook 2 more minutes, stirring frequently.
4. Remove from heat and stir in vanilla.
5. Let stand to cool. Cover with plastic wrap.

Serving Suggestion

The custard can also be used on its own as a dessert, topped with fresh fruit.

Mom's Comfort Food

FOR 6

Turkey Loaf

Skinny Garlic Mashed Potatoes

Roman Salad

Pear Clafouti

Banana Chocolate Chip Muffins

Turkey Loaf

~~~~~~~~~~~~~~~~~~~~~~~~

Oven: 350°F/180°C

1½ lb.	ground turkey	750 g
1 cup	crushed soda crackers	250 mL
½ cup	chopped celery	125 mL
½ cup	chopped onion	125 mL
¼ cup	chopped fresh parsley	50 mL
1	carrot, chopped	1
1 cup	chili sauce or ketchup	250 mL
½ cup	dry white wine or chicken broth	125 mL
1 tbsp.	balsamic vinegar	15 mL
3	egg whites	3
2 tsp.	dried thyme	10 mL
	Salt and pepper to taste	

1. In a large mixing bowl, combine turkey, cracker crumbs, celery, onion, parsley and carrot with half the chili sauce or ketchup.
2. Mix together wine, vinegar, egg whites, thyme, salt and pepper. Add to the turkey mixture.
3. Combine mixture with your hands and mould into a loaf. Place in a baking dish.
4. Spoon remaining chili sauce or ketchup over top.
5. Bake 1 hour or until internal temperature reaches 160°F (70°C). Let stand 15 minutes, then slice and serve.

Skinny Garlic Mashed Potatoes

SERVES 6

~~~~~~~~~~~~~~~~~~~~~~~~~~~~~~~~

4 cups	chicken broth	1 L
2	cloves garlic, crushed	2
10	large potatoes, peeled and cut in pieces	10

1. In a saucepan combine the broth, garlic and potatoes. Cover and bring to a boil. Cook over medium heat until potatoes are tender.
2. Drain potatoes, reserving the broth.
3. Mash the potatoes with 1 to 1¼ cups (250 to 300 mL) of broth, depending on desired consistency.

Roman Salad

~~~~~~~~~~~~~~~~~~~~~~~~~~~~~

½	head romaine, shredded	½
½ cup	chopped dill pickles	125 mL
1	large red onion, sliced in rings	1
	Roman Dressing (below)	

1. In a large salad bowl, combine lettuce, pickles and onion.
2. Drizzle with Roman Dressing and toss.

Roman Dressing

Yields ¼ cup/50 mL

1 tbsp.	olive oil	15 mL
1 tbsp.	water	15 mL
1 tbsp.	lemon juice	15 mL
1	clove garlic, minced	1
½ tsp.	salt	2 mL
	Pepper to taste	

1. Combine all ingredients in a jar and shake well.

Pear Clafouti

~~~~~~~~~~~~~~~~~~~~~~~~~~~~~~~~

Oven: 375°F/190°C

2 cups	cubed peeled pears	500 mL
¾ cup	all-purpose flour	175 mL
¼ tsp.	salt	1 mL
¼ tsp.	nutmeg	1 mL
2 cups	skim milk	500 mL
½ cup	sugar	125 mL
1 tsp.	vanilla	5 mL
1	egg	1
4	lightly beaten egg whites	4
2 tsp.	icing sugar	10 mL

1. Coat a deep 10-inch (25 cm) pie plate with cooking spray and dust with flour.
2. Arrange pear cubes in pie plate. Set aside.
3. Combine flour, salt and nutmeg in a bowl.
4. Gradually add half the milk until well blended.
5. Add the remaining milk, sugar, vanilla, egg and egg whites. Stir until smooth.
6. Pour batter over pears. Bake for 45 minutes or until set.
7. Serve warm or cold. Sift icing sugar over top just before serving. Spoon into bowls to serve.

Banana Chocolate Chip Muffins

Oven: 350°F/180°C

3	large bananas	3
⅔ cup	sugar	150 mL
1	egg	1
1	egg white	1
2 tbsp.	applesauce	30 mL
¼ cup	canola oil	50 mL
1½ cups	all-purpose flour	375 mL
1 tsp.	baking soda	5 mL
1 tsp.	baking powder	5 mL
½ cup	chocolate chips (optional)	125 mL

1. Blend bananas in a food processor. Add sugar, egg, egg white, applesauce and oil. Blend until smooth.
2. Add flour, baking soda and baking powder. Blend well.
3. Stir in chocolate chips (if desired). Spoon into muffin papers in tins.
4. Bake for 20 minutes or until golden and a tester comes out clean.

Après Ski

FOR 6

"Where's the Meat?" Lasagna

Spinach Salad with Beets and Oranges

Sun-Dried Tomato Parmesan Scones

Carrot Cake

"Where's the Meat?" Lasagna

SERVES 6

Oven: 350°F/180°C

1 bag (10 oz.)	fresh spinach	1 bag (284 g)
1 tbsp.	olive oil	15 mL
1½ cups	chopped onion	375 mL
1 cup	sliced mushrooms	250 mL
1	clove garlic, minced	1
2 packages (12 oz.)	Veggie Ground Round	2 packages (375 g)
1⅓ cups	tomato or spaghetti sauce	325 mL
4 tbsp.	chopped fresh parsley	60 mL
1 tbsp.	sugar	15 mL
1 tsp.	dried basil	5 mL
1 tsp.	dried oregano	5 mL
1 tsp.	salt	5 mL
2 cups	no-fat sour cream	500 mL
½ tsp.	Italian seasoning	2 mL
12	lasagna noodles, cooked and drained	12
8	mozzarella-flavour VeggieSlices or shredded low-fat cheese	8

1. Steam spinach for 3 minutes and drain. Cool, chop coarsely and set aside.
2. In a large skillet, sauté onion, mushrooms and garlic in oil.
3. Add Veggie Ground Round; brown for 3 minutes.
4. Add tomato sauce, half of the parsley, sugar, basil, oregano and half of the salt. Simmer for 30 minutes, uncovered and stirring occasionally.
5. Mix together sour cream, remaining parsley, remaining salt, Italian seasoning and chopped spinach.
6. In a 9- x 13-inch (3.5 L) baking dish, layer cooked noodles, veggie tomato mixture, noodles, sour cream mixture, noodles and tomato mixture. Cover with veggie slices.
7. Bake for 45 to 50 minutes or until bubbling. Let stand for 10 minutes.

Preparation Note

Can be made ahead and frozen. To serve, thaw and then bake for 45 to 55 minutes.

A variety of soya meat substitutes are on the market. Readily available is TVP (Textured Vegetable Protein) in fine or coarse varieties to add to spaghetti sauces, soups and so on, as an excellent source of protein. Also available are Yves products such as Veggie Ground Round, which we recommend in this recipe.

Spinach Salad with Beets and Oranges

2	oranges	2
6 cups	torn spinach	1.5 L
3 cups	shredded cooked beets	750 mL
1 tbsp.	olive oil	15 mL
2 tbsp.	minced onion	30 mL
¼ cup	raspberry vinegar	50 mL
	Freshly ground pepper	
¼ cup	chopped fresh chives	50 mL
¼ cup	coarsely chopped walnuts	50 mL

1. Peel oranges and cut each into five crosswise slices.
2. Place spinach on a large platter.
3. Spoon beets onto spinach and arrange orange slices on beets.
4. Heat oil in a small nonstick pan over medium heat. Add onion and sauté until tender.
5. Stir in raspberry vinegar and pepper.
6. Drizzle dressing over salad; sprinkle with chives and walnuts.

Sun-Dried Tomato Parmesan Scones

YIELDS 12 SCONES

Oven: 400°F/200°C

½ cup	boiling water	125 mL
4	sun-dried tomatoes	4
2 cups	all-purpose flour	500 mL
½ cup	grated Parmesan	125 mL
2 tbsp.	sugar	30 mL
1 tsp.	baking powder	5 mL
¾ tsp.	dried oregano	4 mL
½ tsp.	baking soda	2 mL
½ tsp.	salt	2 mL
¾ cup	buttermilk	175 mL
2 tbsp.	olive oil	30 mL
2	egg whites	2

1. Combine boiling water and sun-dried tomatoes in a bowl. Let stand 30 minutes. Drain and finely chop.
2. Combine flour, Parmesan, sugar, baking powder, oregano, baking soda and salt in a separate bowl.
3. Whisk together tomatoes, buttermilk, oil and egg whites in another bowl.
4. Add wet mixture to dry mixture, stirring until the dough is moist. It will be sticky.

(continued)

5. Turn dough out onto a lightly floured surface and knead gently 4 times with floured hands.
6. Pat dough, in a roughly circular shape, to a thickness of 1½ inches (4 cm) onto a baking sheet coated with cooking spray.
7. Cut dough into wedges, cutting into but not through the dough.
8. Bake for 18 minutes or until golden. Cut the wedges all the way through and serve warm or cool on a rack.

Carrot Cake

Oven: 325°C/160°C

1 cup	sugar	250 mL
¼ cup	canola oil	50 mL
2	eggs	2
1	egg white	1
½ cup	applesauce	125 mL
1½ cups	all-purpose flour	375 mL
1½ tsp.	cinnamon	7 mL
1½ tsp.	baking powder	7 mL
1 tsp.	baking soda	5 mL
¼ tsp.	salt	1 mL
2 cups	finely grated carrots	500 mL
¼ cup	chopped Brazil nuts	50 mL
	Icing sugar	
	Cream Cheese Icing	
	(optional, page 314)	

1. Beat sugar and oil in food processor or with electric beaters.
2. Beat in eggs 1 at a time. Beat in egg white and applesauce.
3. Combine flour, cinnamon, baking powder, baking soda and salt in a separate bowl. Fold into the creamed mixture.
4. Fold in carrots and nuts.

(continued)

5. Pour into a greased bundt pan or 2 round 8- or 9-inch (2 or 2.5 L) cake pans. Bake for 35 to 40 minutes for the cake pans, longer for the bundt pan, or until tester comes out clean. Cool in pan for 5 minutes on a rack. Remove from pans to cool.
6. Sprinkle with icing sugar, or use the traditional Cream Cheese Icing (below).

Cream Cheese Icing

8 oz.	light cream cheese, softened	250 g
2 tbsp.	butter	30 mL
2 cups	icing sugar	500 mL
2 tsp.	vanilla	10 mL

1. Cream cheese and butter together.
2. Add icing sugar and vanilla; blend well.

Preparation Note

Pecans or walnuts can be substituted for the Brazil nuts. Try using the ultra low-fat cream cheese for the icing.

Tandoori Treasure

FOR 6

Tandoori Chicken

Fragrant Basmati Rice

(Naan Bread)

Cucumber Salad

Bombay Beans

Crème Caramel

Tandoori Chicken

SERVES 6

~~~~~~~~~~~~~~~~~~~~~~~~~~~~~~~~~~~

Oven: 350°F/180°C

3 lb.	boneless, skinless chicken thighs and breasts	1.5 kg
	Marinade 1 (page 317)	
	Marinade 2 (page 317)	
1 tbsp.	cornstarch	15 mL
2 tbsp.	water	30 mL
	Chopped fresh coriander for garnish	

1. Cut chicken into serving portions. Make shallow cuts in the meat.
2. Rub Marinade 1 evenly over chicken pieces. Place in a sealed container and refrigerate several hours.
3. Make Marinade 2 in a separate bowl. Spoon it over chicken pieces. Marinate for 6 hours or overnight.
4. Remove some of the marinade from the chicken. Place chicken in baking dish and bake for 45 minutes, turning pieces during cooking, until chicken is no longer pink inside. (Can also be barbecued.)
5. Mix cornstarch in water and stir into juice in the bottom of the pan until thickened. Serve sauce separately or pour over chicken on a platter. Garnish with chopped coriander.

Marinade 1

2 tbsp.	lemon juice	30 mL
1 tsp.	minced garlic	5 mL
1 tsp.	salt	5 mL
½ tsp.	Asian chili powder	2 mL
½ tsp.	turmeric	2 mL
	Pinch ground cloves	

1. Mix all ingredients together in a small bowl.

Marinade 2

¾ cup	low-fat plain yogurt	175 mL
2 tbsp.	chopped fresh coriander	30 mL
1 tbsp.	ground cumin	15 mL
2 tsp.	grated fresh ginger	10 mL
1 tsp.	dried mint	5 mL
1 tsp.	white vinegar	5 mL
½ tsp.	cinnamon	2 mL
½ tsp.	ground cardamom	2 mL
¼ tsp.	salt	1 mL

1. Mix all ingredients together in a bowl.

Fragrant Basmati Rice

SERVES 6

3 cups	basmati or long-grain rice	750 mL
1 tsp.	olive oil	5 mL
1	cinnamon stick, broken in half	1
4	cardamom seeds	4
3	cloves	3
	Pinch turmeric	
¼ cup	chopped dried apricots	50 mL
3 ¾ cups	water	925 mL

1. Wash rice. Drain and set aside.
2. Heat oil in saucepan and stir-fry the spices and apricots for several minutes.
3. Add rice and water. Bring to a full boil. Reduce to simmer and cover. Do not stir during cooking. Cook 25 to 30 minutes or until rice is tender. Remove cinnamon sticks before serving.

Cucumber Salad

~~~~~~~~~~~~~~~~~~~~~~~~~~~~

1 can (14 oz.)	pineapple chunks	1 can (398 mL)
½	English cucumber	½
1	small red chili pepper, chopped (optional)	1
3 tbsp.	white vinegar	45 mL
2 tbsp.	sugar	30 mL
1	small onion, sliced	1

1. Pour pineapple, including juice, into a serving bowl.
2. Slice cucumber in quarters lengthwise (leave skin on). Slice pieces and add to bowl.
3. Add chili pepper (if desired), vinegar, sugar and onion. Stir and chill.

Bombay Beans

SERVES 6

~~~~~~~~~~~~~~~~~~~~~~~~~~~~~~

1 tsp.	olive oil	5 mL
1	small onion, chopped	1
1 tsp.	lemon juice	5 mL
½ cup	water	125 mL
1 tsp.	turmeric	5 mL
1 tsp.	ground coriander	5 mL
1 tsp.	Asian chili powder (optional)	5 mL
½ tsp.	sugar	2 mL
	Salt to taste	
3 cups	long green beans	750 mL
2	tomatoes, chopped	2

1. Heat oil in a large skillet. Sauté onion several minutes until golden.
2. Add lemon juice, water, turmeric, coriander and chili powder (if desired). Fry until fragrant, about 1 minute.
3. Add sugar and salt. Bring to a boil. Stir in beans. Boil a few minutes until beans are tender but crunchy.
4. Add tomatoes and cook several minutes longer until heated through.

Crème Caramel

~~~~~~

Oven: 325°F/160°C

1½ cups	sugar	375 mL
¼ cup	water	50 mL
	Pinch cream of tartar	
4	eggs	4
1 tsp.	vanilla	5 mL
¼ tsp.	salt	50 mL
3½ cups	1% milk	875 mL
	Fresh fruit	

1. Place 1 cup (250 mL) of the sugar in a heavy saucepan with the water. Bring to a boil over high heat, stirring until sugar has dissolved. Add cream of tartar and stir with a whisk. Reduce heat to medium and continue to boil, constantly tipping the pot back and forth (but not stirring) until the syrup turns golden brown.

2. Immediately pour the caramel into a stainless steel mould or individual ovenproof custard cups; tilt so the syrup evenly coats sides and bottom of mould. Work quickly. Wear oven mitts, as the mould will become hot.

3. In a large bowl, beat eggs with remaining ½ cup (125 mL) sugar, vanilla and salt.

4. Gradually add milk, beating until smooth.

(continued)

5. Pour custard mixture into mould or cups and place mould in a shallow cake pan. Pour hot water into the pan about 1 inch (2.5 cm) deep. Place the pan on middle rack in oven.
6. Bake 55 to 60 minutes or until knife inserted in custard comes out clean. (Do not overbake, as custard continues to set as it cools.) Remove mould from the pan of hot water and cool completely. Chill for 2 to 3 hours or make day ahead.
7. To unmould, set mould in a pan of hot water for a minute, then loosen edges with spatula. Place serving dish upside down on mould and invert. Shake gently to release custard.
8. Serve chilled with fresh fruit.

Serving Suggestion

This is a wonderfully cooling dessert after a spicy dish. Try serving with fresh mango.

Index

Tomatoes
  Baked Tomatoes with Creamed
    Spinach
  Garlic and Tomato Pepper Kabobs
  Grilled Tomatoes
  Savoury Corn-Filled Tomatoes
  Tomato Stir-Fry
Turnip, Scalloped